MISTER ROGERS'®
PLAY TIME

MISTER ROGERS'

PLAY TIME

**Encourage Your Child to Create,
Explore, and Pretend with Dozens
of Easy-to-Do Activities**

by Fred Rogers

RUNNING PRESS
PHILADELPHIA · LONDON

9   8   7   6   5   4   3   2   1
Digit on the right indicates the number of this printing

Library of Congress Cataloging-in-Publication Number 2001087058

ISBN 0-7624-1123-6

Cover and interior illustrations by Maureen Rupprecht
Cover and interior design by Alicia Freile
Edited by Melissa Wagner
Typography: Century Schoolbook and Frutiger

This book may be ordered by mail from the publisher.
Please include $2.50 for postage and handling.
But try your bookstore first!

Running Press Book Publishers
125 South Twenty-second Street
Philadelphia, Pennsylvania 19103-4399

Visit us on the web!
www.runningpress.com
www.misterrogers.org

Our Thanks to . . .

One of the fortunate things about growing up during the "B.T." (Before Television) era is that I spent much of my childhood playing about all sorts of things. The work on this book has its roots not only in my love of play but also in the appreciation that my parents and grandparents, neighbors and friends had for the everyday playtimes of their childhoods. Healthy, happy childhoods have many, many playtimes.

For me, one of the joys of being a father and a grandfather is being involved in the ways that my sons and grandsons play. I'm grateful to them for giving me another chance to grow in understanding what play can mean to everyone in the family.

During the years that I studied child development, I came to honor play as the "work" of children through my mentors, Dr. Margaret McFarland, Dr. Albert Corrado, and Dr. Nancy Curry. I'm especially thankful for the generous sharing of their insight, their delight, their fascination with the ways that children use play as they grow and learn—and the essential role of the encouraging adult in their development.

Turning our love of playtime into a book for parents became the work of two of our longtime staff members, Hedda Bluestone Sharapan and Cathy Cohen Droz. Their passion for play and their genuine care for the families who would use this book were obvious throughout this project. As I've come to know them and their own families over the years, it's been obvious that they are both parents who value playtime with their own children and who enjoy playfulness in everyday life. Hedda and Cathy love fun, and they obviously love to help others discover it, too. How grateful I am to know them well!

Thanks, too, to our consultant, Dr. Roberta Schomburg, and to a previous staff member and friend, Barry Head, who, through their earlier work with us, have provided an enormous wealth of activities that could inform this present work. We're grateful to Karin Haug, our summer intern, who brought a fresh approach to our discussions. And thanks also to one of our staff members, Britanny Loggi-Smith, and her family, who graciously offered to follow some of the recipes and activities to ensure that our directions were clear and accurate. What's more, they shared the "fruits" of their cooking with all of us at Family Communications, Inc.—delicious!

Our friends at Running Press, especially Melissa Wagner, our editor, and Alicia Freile, our designer, gave their careful, caring attention as we all worked together to make this a helpful book for families. And we were especially pleased to have been able to work again with an old friend, Maureen Rupprecht, who illustrated this book with her usual sensitive artistry.

Everyone at our small nonprofit company, Family Communications, Inc., has contributed in some way to this book, as they do with all our projects. Their dedication in helping provide what's meaningful for children and their pleasure in the playfulness of the lives of their families is an on-going inspiration to me. We all hope that you and your children will continue to delight in growing through the playtimes of your lives.

Table of Contents

Introduction

"Child's play" is one of the most misleading phrases in our language. People often use it to suggest something trivial, but a child's play is not trivial—not by any means. When children play, they're working. They're working on learning about themselves, about other people, and about the world around them. Playtime is one of the most important times for children to learn and grow.

When I watch children play, I get particular pleasure from seeing them use whatever they have to play with in unexpected ways. A child who uses an empty wrapping paper tube as a tunnel for little cars to go through, or a towel for a teddy bear's blanket, is a creative child, a discoverer, and a problem-solver. Playtime in childhood can be the root of life-long abilities that help us to cope, to learn, and to become all that we can be.

Playtime for learning—and fun

A letter came to us a while ago that said so much to me about playtime and parenting.

"I'm a 28-year-old mother. I've been feeling the responsibility of being a parent very heavily. . . . So I've bought books and books and books. I felt sure that if I didn't do exactly right as a parent, my son would suffer. By his second birthday, I made sure he could count to twelve and recognize all the letters of the alphabet.

". . . I've since come to realize that my son needed to be a child, and that I needed him to be one. Now that means more to me than trying to store information in his ever-expanding brain. It means letting him enjoy life as only a child can, with the sheer enjoyment of the wonders of this world, however small they may be. Did you know you can see rainbows on the wings of common houseflies?

"This afternoon my son and I pretended to be different kinds of animals, laughing a lot. Then we got tired, so we sat at the table and made a pinwheel. My son didn't learn about the ABCs or numbers, but he was learning to pretend and play for fun."

I would venture a guess that, at the same time, her son was learning all sorts of important things—things that would help him in school, like imagination, sticking to a task, following directions, paying attention—and feeling good about himself and his relationship with others.

She continued in her letter,

"At last I feel like I've been given permission to be the kind of parent I want to be. I'm not a teacher. I'm a mom, and an imperfect mom at that, with fears and hopes and dreams like anyone else—but with an awful lot of love inside for my little boy."

Her comments reminded me of something essential that I learned from Helen Ross, a remarkable teacher in child development and a consultant for the *Neighborhood* programs— DON'T FORGET THE FUN!

About this book

Besides offering fun and meaningful activities, we wanted to make this book easy for parents to use. We've organized the activities in chapters, using categories that are of interest to children or characteristics that parents want to encourage.

In every chapter we've offered a variety of activities—

ideas for what to do with food, crafts, music, movement, and outdoor play. You know your child best, so you're the best one to decide which activities your child might enjoy.

You might also want to use the index in which we've listed each type of activity. For example, if it's a nice day for outdoor playtime, you'll find the outside activities listed together in the index. Or, if it's a rainy day, you may want to look in the index to find a kitchen or craft idea.

When we made our selections for this book, we particularly kept in mind how busy parents are these days. We specifically chose ideas that take little preparation, are easy for children to do, and require only readily available household materials.

Some children may need extra help getting started, so we've included some suggestions. For example, if your child is stumped about what kind of picture to draw or dance to create, you could say, "How about 'one of your favorite places?'" or "a terrible day?" or "the best birthday party?" When we encourage children to bring something relevant from their own lives to their play, we're helping them reach into their uniqueness and express something that's meaningful for them.

Getting started

Start with what your child enjoys doing. Does your child spend a lot of time playing with toy cars? Maybe he or she likes to explore things outdoors. Or maybe you have a child who always seems to reach for a pencil or crayon to draw things. Turn to the chapters that feel like a good fit for your child.

You could also start with what you want to encourage in your child, like cooperation, help with chores around the house, talking about feelings, or developing an appreciation for nature.

You might want to look for the kind of play you like to do, too. What did you enjoy as a child? Which chapter of this book catches your eye? Your enthusiasm for a particular kind of play will most likely make it more attractive for your child.

During one of my first practicum courses in Child Development at the University of Pittsburgh, I saw firsthand how much children's play can be affected by an adult. I was observing four-year-olds at the Family and Children's Center. The director of the center had invited a well-known sculptor to come to visit. The director said to the sculptor, "I'd like you simply to love working with your clay in front of the children—not teach them technique. Just love what you do in front of them." Well, that sculptor did just that, and little by little, those four year olds started doing their own unique things with clay—not as an assignment, but because they caught the notion that they could find satisfaction in using clay just as their guest did. That sculptor came to visit those young children once a week for the whole semester. Not before or since have that center's four-year-olds used the medium of clay so imaginatively.

That story reminds me of the Quaker saying, "Attitudes are caught, not taught." When you do with your child whatever you love to do, or even when you just talk about those things with your heartfelt appreciation, that's contagious!

Setting limits

When we introduce a playtime idea to a child, we often need to provide some limits, especially if we're indoors or in our homes. No one wants furniture or walls messed up.

Before you start the play, it's a good idea to let your child know about the rules, like "newspaper goes on the table before you paint" or "the clay stays on the table." Putting play clay on a cookie sheet might even be more helpful, so your child sees and feels where the clay needs to stay.

It can also help if you remind your child before you start playing that there will be clean-up time afterward. Then about ten minutes before you need to end the play, let your child know clean-up is coming soon. Clean-up time is a natural part of playtime.

There can be wonderful benefits, too, when we make limits on what our children can do. I remember watching a toddler whose mother had just told her to stop putting a pen into her mouth. From the look on the little girl's face, you could see she had a problem: how to please her mother and yet satisfy her urge to play with the pen. She solved her problem by finding a hole in the side of a toy—and for several minutes she played contentedly, poking the pen through the hole, dropping it, picking it up, and poking it through again.

Watching that happen helped me realize how important limits are for the development of children's creativity. When we won't let them do exactly what they want to do, they have the opportunity of creating new alternatives.

Parents and playtime

How much or how little you get involved in these activities depends on you, on your child's needs and abilities, and on the situation. For some of these activities and for some children, you may need only to set out the materials. The play will take hold, and you can step back.

When you're more involved, you're likely to find that it's more than "playtime" that happens. A friend of mine was sitting at the kitchen table and spotted an empty egg carton on the counter. He decided to make something from it that he remembered from his own childhood. His four-year-old daughter was in the next room, watching television, but at one point she wandered into the kitchen to see what was going on.

She asked her father what he was doing, and he told her, "I thought I'd see if I could make a toy car." When she asked, "Why?" he answered, "Just for fun. I used to make them from egg cartons when I was a boy."

She thought about that for a moment and asked if she could help. Her father invited her to sit by him and told her he could use some help. Half an hour went by, and little by little, the father helped his daughter do as much of the project as she was able to do. When it was done, she picked up the egg-carton car and ran upstairs to her mother and cried out, "Look, Mommy! Look what Daddy and I just made!" Just think about how much it meant to her—on many levels—to have that playtime with her father, building something together, appreciating each other's creative ideas, and feeling proud of what they made. And think about how much that playtime must have meant to her father, too!

Whenever you become involved, whether you're watching the play as an interested bystander or becoming a partner with your child in the play, you'll have a wonderful opportunity to learn more about your child— and probably more about yourself, too.

You may also find that by watching your child at play, you'll tap into some of the playfulness inside you, remembering your childhood and discovering new things about yourself. Parenting gives us many chances to grow right along with our growing children.

Sharing
and Caring

Encouraging cooperation and kindness

Sharing and caring go hand in hand. They're both hard for most children, but that doesn't mean those children are spoiled or uncooperative or unkind. It just means that they're human.

Friends of mine told me a story about something that happened on a day when their daughter Michelle had a friend over for the afternoon. The girls wanted to play outside, but the afternoon air was cool. Michelle threw a tantrum after her parents offered one of her sweaters to the friend. It wasn't a particular favorite of Michelle's, so they couldn't understand why she made such a fuss! They seemed to be asking me, "How did we raise such a selfish kid?"

Michelle's angry response to her parents' lending her sweater to her playmate was not unusual, and it was not the mark of an uncaring child. Most children have trouble sharing. Being able to share and to care happens through a long process. Even though we can't expect most preschoolers will always share, cooperate, and care about other people's feelings, there are things that we can do to encourage them in that direction.

Sharing from children's perspective

First, we can try to understand what sharing means from their point of view. To a young child, what's "me" is "mine" and what's "mine" is "me." You've probably heard a child say "me chair," instead of "my chair." No wonder it's hard for them to share—if sharing means giving up a part of "me."

A mother of a preschooler found that when her son was in control of when and what he would share, he was much more receptive to sharing his toys. The mother suggested to her son that he allow a friend to play with a certain toy when he was finished with it, and usually found that her son would hand over the toy after only a few moments more. I have a hunch that children are much more willing to "share" when they feel they're in control.

A kitchen timer is another way some parents help their children with taking turns. A timer is a neutral timekeeper, so children trust that when they give up a toy to another child, they will get it back after a certain amount of time.

Holding on vs. letting go

Before children can let go of something to share it, they need to know what it means to hold on to something, or own it. That's why it can help children to have some things that they don't have to share, like their favorite soft animal or blanket. Before a friend comes to play, it may be a good idea to let your child decide which toys he or she will be willing to let someone else play with. You might want to suggest that your child put away the toys that are just too personal to share.

One of the most difficult things for children to share is the attention of their parents, but when children can trust they will have their parents' undivided attention, even for a little bit of time each day, they are more likely to be able to share their parents at other times.

Developing empathy

Caring, too, grows little by little as children develop the ability to see the world through other people's eyes. That's the foundation for empathy, the capacity to appreciate how others might feel.

We can help children become more aware of others' needs by praising them when they share a toy or a snack or when they comfort someone who is hurt or crying. It helps to be on the look-out for such times. Your actions help your child to know that you appreciate such expressions of kindness. When you say to your child "You're really growing," you're helping to make it clear that we grow inside as well as outside.

Another thing we can do is to offer activities, like the ones in this chapter, that let children know first-hand that there's fun and value in sharing and caring. They'll learn, little by little, that great good comes from both.

Paper Chains

One child working alone can't make a very long chain, but if another child gets involved, that chain will grow . . . and grow . . . and grow!

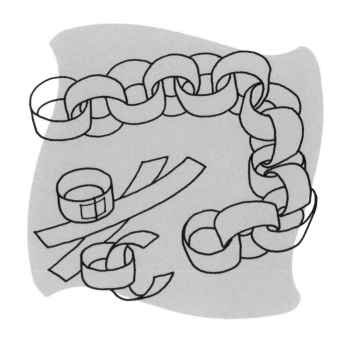

YOU'LL NEED:
Assortment of colored construction paper
Blunt-nosed scissors
Glue or tape

* Show the children how to cut the construction paper into strips suitable for making small loops. Make a loop from a construction paper strip and tape or glue it together. Then show the children how to thread a second loop through the first to make a chain. The children might enjoy the challenge of making the chain as long as the whole room.

* When the chain is finished, hang it up with masking tape, and you've got a homemade decoration for a birthday or holiday—or a way to make an ordinary day all the more festive.

YOUR CHILD IS WORKING ON:
Teamwork
Dexterity

A Silly Folded Picture

Here's an idea that's no fun to do alone—your child will need at least one other partner, but it works even better with three.

YOU'LL NEED:
Sheets of paper
Pencil, pen, or marker

* Fold a sheet of paper in thirds, so that only the top third is showing.

* Out of view of the others, have your child draw the head of an animal or person on the top third. Then ask your child to fold that section under to hide what he or she has drawn.

* The next person sees only the middle third, where he or she will draw the body of the person or animal. Fold the picture so the top two-thirds are hidden, and pass it on to someone else.

* The last person will draw the legs of the animal or person.

* Unfold the picture to find a funny group masterpiece!

YOUR CHILD IS WORKING ON:
Appreciating other people's ideas
Dexterity
Imagination

Taking Turns

Like most games, this one gives children practice at taking turns. Since it also involves reading words and numbers, the children will probably need help from you or an older child.

YOU'LL NEED:
Blunt-nosed scissors
Cardboard or heavy paper
Brass paper fastener
Marker
Paper or index cards

Make a spinner: Cut a 5- or 6-inch circle or square from cardboard or heavy paper and divide it into sections, writing a number in each section. Make a 3-inch arrow from the leftover cardboard and attach it to the circle using a brass paper fastener. Loosen the arrow if necessary so it spins easily.

✳ Cut paper into 3 x 5-inch pieces to use as instruction cards. Ask the children to think of activities to write on the cards. Here are a few suggestions:

>   Clap your hands
>   Whisper "no, thank you"
>   Turn around
>   Touch your toes
>   Shout "yes, please"
>   Say your name
>   Knock on the door

✳ Mix up the cards. Have a child pick a card, then spin the spinner to see how many times to do what the card says. For example, if the spinner stops on four and the card says "Say your name," the child will say his or her name four times.

YOUR CHILD IS WORKING ON:
Taking turns
Patience
Literacy
Number recognition

A Clothespin Cooperation Game

With this game, children can see that some things can't get accomplished unless they work together.

YOU'LL NEED:
3 or 4 clothespins (the spring type)
String, yarn, or clothesline
Plastic milk jug with a narrow opening

✳ Tie pieces of yarn onto the clothespins (one for each child) and put the clothespins inside the milk jug with only the strings hanging out.

✳ Tell the children to pull the clothespins from the jar. What happens if they all try to pull at the same time? Can they think of a way to get the clothespins out?

YOUR CHILD IS WORKING ON:
Cooperation
Taking turns
Patience
Dexterity

This activity can open the door for discussions about other times when children need to cooperate. For example, what can they do when two children want the same cup? What if they want to play with the same toy? How can they solve those kinds of problems peacefully?

Room to Share

When you unfurl a long roll of paper and show the children they have a big area to draw on, they'll realize that they can work side by side and end up with a much bigger and more interesting mural than any one child can draw alone.

YOU'LL NEED:
A long piece of paper from a roll of plain
  shelf paper
Markers or crayons
Tape

* Unroll the paper to the length of the work area (the floor or a table). You'll probably need to use tape to hold the ends down.

* Help the children decide how to work together by asking questions like:

> How can we decide where each
>   person should draw?
> Should each person draw a part of
>   one picture, or should each draw
>   his or her own picture?
> Do they want to use a theme?
>   Maybe the ocean, a garden, the
>   circus, or a house and yard?

* Once the children have come to an agreement, set out the crayons or markers, and let them get to work.

* This could be a fun way to make a birthday banner for a friend or for someone in the family. What an interesting way to say "we care about you."

YOUR CHILD IS WORKING ON:
Cooperation
Creativity
Decision-making
Appreciating other people's ideas

> **Be sure to comment with an encouraging word when the children are working well together. They probably aren't going to get along all the time, but when you praise the cooperative moments, you're helping your child know you value cooperation.**

Fishing for Words

Watch your child practice taking turns, work on imagination and dexterity, and appreciate reading while playing this fishing game with one or more friends.

YOU'LL NEED:
Magnet
String
Pencil or ruler
Fish shapes cut from heavy paper
Paper clips
Bucket or dish pan

* Tie a magnet to a piece of string, then fasten the string to a pencil or ruler to make a fishing rod.

* Your child may be able to help draw or cut fish shapes from heavy paper and place paper clips on them.

* On each fish, write an activity for your child to do. Here are some suggestions for pretending:

> Pretend to be a baby
> Pretend to walk like a very tall person
> Pretend to be an animal
> Pretend to be a dancer

* Put all of the fish into the bucket or dish pan. Have the children try to catch the fish with the rod—it might take a while to get one. When a child's rod catches a fish, he or she does the activity written on the fish, and then waits for his or her next turn while the other children go fishing.

YOUR CHILD IS WORKING ON:
Taking turns
Persistence
Patience
Pretending
Literacy

A Pizza Factory

Here's a meal that can be done as an assembly line, with everyone sharing in the work.

YOU'LL NEED:
Bagels or English muffins (cut or split in half)
Bowls for toppings
Tomato sauce
Mozzarella cheese slices
Pizza toppings (i.e. mushrooms, olive slices,
    green peppers, etc.)
Mixing spoon
Cookie sheet

* Lay out the ingredients in a line on the table, so that each child will have his or her own work space.

* With input from the children, decide who will do the tasks that will be necessary to make the individual pizzas, including:

> Spread the sauce
> Tear the cheese into shreds
> Put the cheese onto the pizzas
> Put on the additional toppings
> Put the pizzas on to the cookie sheet

* Let the children know that for safety reasons, an adult needs to be the one to put the cookie sheet under the broiler or in a toaster oven. The pizzas are done when the cheese melts.

* Once the pizzas are ready, everyone can enjoy the fruits of their labor, thanks to the cooperation of the assembly line!

YOUR CHILD IS WORKING ON:
Teamwork
Dexterity
Making healthy food choices

A Caring Center

For young children, it can be such a good feeling to be the one who's giving the care.

YOU'LL NEED:
Baby dolls or stuffed animals
Small blankets or towels
Dress-up clothes (vest, purse, briefcase, tie)
Doll clothes (optional)
Baby bottle or spoon (optional)
Washcloths and masking tape for diapers

✳ Getting the play started probably won't take much more than stuffed animals or baby dolls and something that's like a blanket. Some children like to dress-up when they play mommies and daddies. For them, you might want to bring out grownup play-clothes, like vests, ties, aprons, purses, briefcases, etc. You might also make a swinging cradle by tying or pinning a sheet between two chairs.

✳ If the children need help getting started, you can ask what kinds of things mothers and fathers do to help take care of a baby— holding and rocking the baby; feeding the baby; changing the baby's diaper; telling the baby nursery rhymes; playing peek-a-boo; showing the baby rattles or toys.

✳ Think about how much it can mean to your child when you say something like, "Your baby is lucky to have such a caring parent."

YOUR CHILD IS WORKING ON:
Kindness
Developing a nurturing attitude
Role-playing

> When children play about being care-givers for dolls or stuffed animals, they practice thinking of others' needs and doing specific tasks to care for them. Children are likely to take that good feeling of caring into everyday life.

Mirror Images

Preschoolers are naturally egocentric, but in this activity they need to focus on another person's face, gestures, and movements. Your child's partner can be another child or an adult.

YOU'LL NEED:
A partner

* Have the partners stand in pairs, facing each other—as if they're looking in a mirror.

* One person starts as the leader. As the leader moves, the follower imitates that movement.

* At some point, change roles, so that each partner has the chance to be leader and follower.

YOUR CHILD IS WORKING ON:
Empathy
Observation skills
Taking turns
Coordination

In times of conflict, when your child has done something that upsets a friend, you could ask your child to look at his or her friend's face, just like your child did for this activity. Paying attention to other people's facial expressions or movements can help children realize that the things they do really affect others.

Thank-You Cards

"Thank you" may well be the most important phrase in the English language! Help your child develop an attitude of gratitude with this activity.

YOU'LL NEED:
Paper or an index card
Pencils, markers, or crayons
Magazine pictures or stickers (optional)
Glue (optional)
Envelope

✳ Fold the paper or index card in half to make a card.

✳ With your help, have your child think about someone who has done something nice or helpful for him or her. The card could be addressed to:

Parent, brother, or sister
Grandparent, neighbor, or friend
Babysitter, child-care provider,
    or preschool teacher
Mail carrier
Crossing guard

✳ Ask your child what kind of thank you message he or she would like to write in the card. A younger child might dictate the words to you. Older children may be able to write a message or sign their own names.

✳ Have your child decorate the front of the card with a drawing, magazine pictures, or stickers.

YOUR CHILD IS WORKING ON:
Expression of appreciation to others
Creativity
Literacy
Dexterity

Pretend Play

Developing imagination

A preschooler we know spent much of his playtime pretending to be a superhero. He was small for his age, spoke in a quiet voice, and was often shy when he met someone new, but once he had his cape on, he talked with a deep, strong voice, and he walked with a swagger. Just how much that costume meant to him became obvious to his family when he insisted on wearing his cape to the doctor's office. It seemed to help him feel braver and stronger—and made his visit to the doctor more manageable.

When children pretend, they aren't limited to the way things are in the real world. They're using their imagination to move beyond the bounds of reality. A stick can be a magic wand. A sock can be a puppet. A small child can be a powerful superhero, a crying baby, a mean dragon, or a scary lion—whatever he or she wants to be.

Trying on feelings

Although pretending can take many different forms, much of it seems to be a way for children to find out how they feel about something. Playing out different roles is a way for children to begin to understand other people's feelings, too. Seeing things from another person's point of view can be particularly hard for young children. Role playing can help them feel what it may be like to be another person for a little while.

Power and independence

One of the fascinating things about growing is how we move from dependence to independence. How dependent and independent children are—and how dependent and independent they want to be—is one of the biggest struggles of our earliest years. While children are often arguing about wanting to be in complete charge, they really don't want to be in charge because it would be too scary for them. Nevertheless, they can play about being in charge. In their play, children can put their toys and pretend people in different situations and make them act in ways they can't control real people or real big things around them. They play "all grown up!" Don't be surprised, though, if in the next moment they're playing about being the baby!

Understanding what's real and what's pretend

Sometimes pretending can seem so real that children wonder if putting on a costume might actually change them inside. It's important for them to know that although we can pretend to be someone else, we can never be someone else. We will always be ourselves.

Encouraging imagination

Whenever you encourage your child's imagination, you're also stretching your child's thinking skills. Young children know best what they see, hear, smell, or touch. That's concrete thinking. But when they use their imagination for their pretend play, they're using abstract thinking, and that's essential for school learning and for creative thinking and problem-solving all through life.

Parents sometimes wonder how much they ought to offer or suggest to stimulate imagination. The best kind of playthings are open-ended materials, like dress-up clothes, puppets, and art materials, because children can use them to work through their thoughts

and feelings about the world. Some children need specific play props at times, like a toy telephone. Others may be satisfied if you just put your hand to your ear, pretending to talk on the phone. As you become an active partner in your child's imaginary play, you will come to know your child better, and you'll have a better sense of what might be helpful.

Grown-Up Play

Children especially like to imagine what it's like to be the grownups who are important in their lives—that's why they often play about being moms and dads.

YOU'LL NEED:
Any or all of the following:
- Purses
- Jewelry
- Hats
- Old briefcase
- Old nightgown
- Baby doll
- Baby bottle
- Blanket

YOUR CHILD IS WORKING ON:
Role-playing
Playing about power
Developing a nurturing attitude

✳ Some children see dress-up clothes and props and they immediately begin elaborate pretend play. Other children may need some help getting started. You might suggest a situation close to what your child has experienced. For example, pretend that there is a sick baby in the house or your child is a new babysitter who needs to learn the baby's routine. Familiar themes like that can make the best starters for dramatic play.

> **While some children want to play about being the grownups, other children might want to be the babies. Sometimes the stresses of growing are hard, and children like to have a break by pretending to be the baby, wanting someone to take care of them.**

Cape Play

Just putting on a cape can be enough of a prop to help your child play about all sorts of powerful roles: a king or queen or superhero.

YOU'LL NEED:
Soft blanket, large scrap of fabric, or a
   big towel
Large safety pin
Crown, jewelry (optional)
Magic wand (optional)
Deck of cards (optional)

✳ Pin the blanket, fabric, or towel loosely around your child's neck. What kind of play does the cape start for your child? You might suggest one of the following scenarios:

Royal Play: Your child might want to be a king or queen and plan a royal banquet for a meal. Show your child how to bow or curtsy to the guests (who might be friends, relatives, or even stuffed animals!). How might people eat in a fancy way? What might they say to each other? You might want to play some majestic sounding music, like Tchaikovsky's or Prokofiev's *Romeo and Juliet* ballets. Your child might enjoy commanding his or her "subjects" to do certain things—especially if you're the one who is pretending to obey his or her commands.

Superhero Play: Being powerful superheroes can be especially enticing play as children become more independent, yet still recognize that grownups control when they go to bed, when and what they eat, etc. This kind of play sometimes leads to chase-and-rescue running that can get out of hand. It can help your child to know ahead of time that you'll stop the play if someone might get hurt.

YOUR CHILD IS WORKING ON:
Using play to work on feeling powerful
Understanding the difference between
   real and pretend

Abracadabra

Some children delight in playing the role of a magician.

YOU'LL NEED:
Large sheet of black paper
Tape
Stapler
Blunt-nosed scissors
Strip of cardboard or stick
Glue
Glitter
Black cape, dark towel, or material (optional)

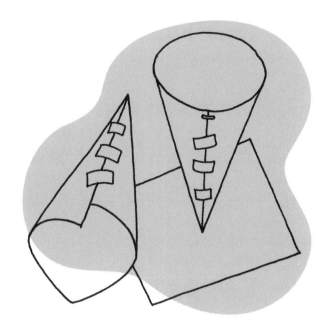

* To make a magician's hat, roll the paper into a cone shape with a point at one end. Tape the pointed end together and staple the bottom edge to fit your child's head. Cut off the extra paper at the bottom to make a straight edge.

* Make a magic wand by gluing glitter to the end of a strip of cardboard or stick.

* You might also want to offer a black cape, or a piece of black material or a dark towel to use as a cape.

* Your child might want to do pretend magic tricks. So much of the world is magical to young children. The very simplest "disappearing" tricks can be fun, and sometimes just pretending to have magical powers can be enough.

YOUR CHILD IS WORKING ON:
Playing about power
Understanding the difference between
    real and pretend

I Crown Thee King or Queen

Royal robes and glittery crowns can make your child feel grand, powerful, and very fancy.

YOU'LL NEED:

Strips of construction paper or lightweight cardboard about 4"–8" wide

Blunt-nosed scissors

Scrap craft materials (feathers, yarn, buttons)

Aluminum foil

Foil wrapping paper or metallic ribbon

Sequins or glitter (optional)

Glue

Tape

Majestic music (optional)

Food for a royal feast (optional)

* Tape two strips of paper together to make a crown that fits your child's head.

* Your child may need help cutting points or fringe along the top of the crown. Then your child can decorate with scrap materials, markers, small pieces of aluminum foil, foil wrapping paper, or metallic ribbon. Your child might also want to glue on sequins or sprinkle glitter over glue that has been drizzled on the crown.

* Fasten the headband around your child's head.

* Once your child is bedecked in these fancy things, you might want to greet him or her with a curtsy or bow, play some majestic music for a dance, or offer a feast to be eaten with royal table manners.

YOUR CHILD IS WORKING ON:

Feeling powerful

Developing imagination

Creativity

Pretending

An Imaginary Land

Here's imaginary play that starts with just one simple prop, a key, so you can do this anywhere—in the car, in a waiting room, or at home on a rainy day.

YOU'LL NEED:
Key or a key made out of cardboard

* Give your child the key and say something like "Let's pretend this key opens the door to an imaginary land." Let your child pretend to open a door with the key.

* You could ask questions like: What do you see when you open the door? Who is meeting you and taking you on a tour of this imaginary land? What is happening there?

YOUR CHILD IS WORKING ON:
Imagination
Pretending

As an active partner in this kind of imaginary play, you can encourage your child to rely more and more on his or her own imagination. It's hard for parents to know how much to elaborate. The more your child does, the less you'll need to do. Talking about imaginary things might remind you of your own childhood, and your child will probably love to hear about that.

What's Cooking?

With a chef hat and play dough or paper, your child can pretend to whip up a fabulous meal or dessert.

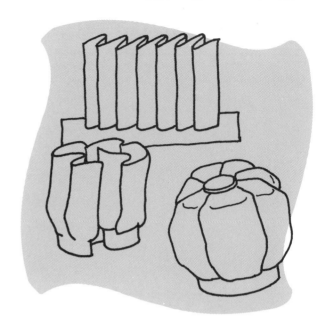

YOU'LL NEED:
20" x 30" piece of tissue or
    construction paper
Glue or staples
Cardboard strip 2" wide and just
    a little longer than the circumference
    of your child's head
Construction paper
Blunt-nosed scissors
Paper plates
Crayons or colored markers
Play clay (see recipe on page 92)

✳ Pleat a piece of tissue or construction paper and glue the pleated edge to the cardboard.

✳ Join the cardboard band and the pleated paper with glue or staples.

✳ Close the top of the hat by gluing a 3-inch circle of construction paper to the open sides of the crepe paper.

✳ Your child might want to use the play clay or construction paper to make pretend food like burgers, cakes, or cookies.

YOUR CHILD IS WORKING ON:
Creativity
Role-playing
Following directions

Paper Bag Hats

Save those paper bags—they make great-looking wigs or hats!

YOU'LL NEED:
Medium-sized paper bag
Blunt-nosed scissors
Construction paper scraps, yarn bits,
   or buttons
Glue

* To make a paper bag wig, cut away the front part of the bag, leaving some of the paper in the front to make bangs. Cut the paper bag into thin strips all the way around. If you like, you can roll the strips of paper around a pencil to make them curl, or add flowers, ribbon, bows, or other hair decoration to make the wig fancy.

* Here's a way to make a hat: Turn the bag inside out, leaving a turned-up cuff on the outside. Scrunch the bag into any shape. Let your child decorate it with yarn, paint, or markers. Your child could also dab it with glue and add paper or fabric scraps, buttons, and just about anything else to decorate the hat.

YOUR CHILD IS WORKING ON:
Creativity
Imagination

Dancing to Music

Music can sound like romping elephants or blowing wind. Listen to instrumental classical or jazz music and watch your child's imagination soar—and arms and legs dance.

YOU'LL NEED:
Music
   Musical suggestions: Saint-Saens' "Carnival of the Animals," *Fantasia* Soundtrack, Tchaikovsky's "Nutcracker Suite"
Streamer, scarf, or towel

＊ Play music on a CD, tape, or radio and ask your child to listen and think about what kind of animal or feeling the music sounds like. Ask your child to move or dance the way he or she thinks the music sounds. Your child might want to pretend about these ideas with the streamer or scarf:

> an elephant with a long trunk
> the blowing wind
> a butterfly
> a tightrope walker

＊ Play music with a different tempo and feeling and invite your child to dance in a way that matches the new music.

YOUR CHILD IS WORKING ON:
Coordination
Listening skills
Pretending
Imagination

Puppet Play

Puppets come in many forms, shapes, and sizes. Because they're held an arm's length away, they can take on personalities of their own. At a comfortable distance, the puppets are really parts of a child's own personality that might not otherwise be expressed.

On the pages that follow, you'll find ideas for several kinds of homemade puppets. Here are some suggestions to help your child get comfortable with puppet play:

* Start by talking **about** the puppet—what it is, what it's made of, how it feels, what kind of puppet it might be.

* Slip the puppet on your hand or hold it and begin talking **to** the puppet, telling it about your child or something that has happened that day.

* As your child becomes more interested in the puppet's reaction, then you can begin talking **for** the puppet, answering the questions you ask, and turning the puppet to talk with your child as well.

* When your child seems comfortable, let your child have his or her puppet talk to yours.

* Here are a few suggestions to get puppet play started. The best stories are generally the ones that come from you and your child as you play together.

> Everyday experiences in a puppet family as they wake up, eat, or do other daily routines
>
> Taming a scary puppet
>
> A new child comes to your neighborhood
>
> The puppet is worried about starting school
>
> The puppet doesn't want to go to bed

YOUR CHILD IS WORKING ON:
Creativity
Imagination
Using play to work on feelings
Pretending

Spoon Puppets

YOU'LL NEED:
Wooden spoon or large serving spoon
Markers
Scrap craft materials
   (yarn, felt, cotton balls, paper, etc.)
Glue
Handkerchief or square of material
   (5 or 6 square inches)
Ribbon or yarn

✱ An easy spoon puppet can be made by just
drawing faces on either side of the spoon,
or gluing on bits of felt or scrap paper.
Yarn or cotton balls glued to the top of
the spoon can become hair.

✱ For a more elaborate puppet, cover the
spoon handle with a handkerchief or
square of material, fastening it in place on
the neck of the spoon with ribbon or yarn.

Stick Puppets

YOU'LL NEED:
Small paper plates
Crayons or markers
Straws, popsicle sticks, or tongue depressors
Scrap craft materials (yarn, paper, fabric,
   buttons, etc.)
Glue
Magazine pictures or drawings (optional)

✱ Have your child draw faces on small paper
plates and then decorate them with scrap
materials. For example, buttons can be eyes
and yarn can be hair. Your child might want
to decorate several plates with different
facial expressions to show different feelings.

✱ Attach the paper plates to straws, tongue
depressors, or popsicle sticks to make
puppets.

✱ Your child can make another kind of stick
puppet by taping a drawing or magazine
picture to a stick.

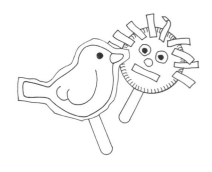

Paper Cup Puppets

YOU'LL NEED:

Paper cup

Scrap craft materials
  (buttons, yarn, paper, etc.)

Markers

* Put the paper cup on your child's finger.

* Make a hole in the paper cup big enough for your child to poke a finger through— the finger will be the puppet's nose.

* Use buttons, yarn, or paper to make the puppet's other features, or your child can draw on the cup with markers or crayons.

* To make simple clothes for the puppet, make three holes in a piece of cloth big enough for your child's thumb, pointer, and third finger to fit through. Put the cloth over your child's hand, and stick your child's pointer finger into the hole in the paper cup. Your child's thumb and third finger can act as the puppet's hands.

Sock Puppets

YOU'LL NEED:

Sock

Scrap craft materials (buttons, paper,
  fabric, yarn, etc.)

Glue

* Show your child how to slip a sock over his or her hand, with knuckles in the heel.

* Make a mouth by tucking the toe end between your fingers and thumb.

* Sew or glue on scrap materials to make eyes, nose, and hair. Be sure to let the glue dry before your child uses the puppet.

Puff Ball
Finger Puppets

YOU'LL NEED:
Cotton balls
Felt, handkerchief, or other fabric
Yarn or pipe cleaner
Popsicle stick or unsharpened pencil
Paper scraps, buttons
Glue
Markers

* Cover several cotton balls with a piece of felt, a handkerchief, or fabric.

* Gather the material below the puff ball with yarn or a pipe cleaner to make the neck. Tie the neck loosely so your child will be able to slip the puppet head over a finger, or attach it to a popsicle stick.

* Have your child draw simple features on the puppet's face with a marker, or cut the features from paper or felt and sew or glue them on the puppet.

* Some children like to make two or three finger puppets, so they can pretend to make them talk to one another.

Pretending with puppets is often a safe way for children to talk about things that concern them. They will sometimes allow puppets to say or do things they would never say or do themselves. Behind this safe facade, they can test out their feelings and our reactions. Whether it's puppets or other kinds of playthings, whatever you and your child create together takes on more significance because of its association with you and your relationship.

Box Puppets

YOU'LL NEED:

Small empty box (pudding, gelatin, or
single-serving cereal box)
Knife or scissors
Tape
Construction paper
Scrap craft materials (buttons, yarn,
cotton balls, etc.)
Markers
Glue

* If you opened the box through a top flap,
tape it shut again. Then cut the box around
the middle on three sides.

* Fold the box along the fourth side to make
a hinge that looks like a mouth.

* Show your child that his or her fingers will
fit in the top part of the box, and place his
or her thumb in the bottom to make the
mouth open and shut.

* Have your child cover the box with pieces
of construction paper and glue on scrap
materials to make a face, hair, and mouth.

Younger children are often fascinated with puppets with mouths because they can use the puppets to pretend about talking, and also about other things like biting and gobbling people up. One task of growing up is learning to use our teeth to chew food, but not to bite other people. Most small children are likely to have angry times when they feel like biting, but little by little, they can tame those feelings, often by letting them out in puppet play.

Helping

Working on responsibility

One day the "Neighborhood" mail contained a particularly delightful surprise—a package of messages from a preschool class. The teacher had asked the children to draw and talk about what makes them feel happy and what makes them feel sad. She told them she'd send the messages on to me.

Among them was this treasure from a young girl who said, "I'm happy when I get mom the toilet paper when she calls out from the bathroom!" No wonder she was happy—she was asked to do something she was able to do, and something that her mother obviously appreciated.

When children know their help is valuable, they feel valued, and naturally they're likely to do helpful things for us and for others in the future.

Taking on responsibility

When babies are young, they depend on us to take care of practically all of their needs. We're the "helpers." Then comes a moment, usually in toddlerhood, when children grab the spoon to feed themselves or insist on trying to dress themselves. "Me do it!" The food may be in more places than the mouth. The shirt may be on backwards, the pants sideways, the socks dangling off the toes, but how proud children are when they find out they can take care of some of their own needs, no matter how primitive their attempts may be!

With our encouragement, little by little children can take on more and more responsibility for themselves. They can begin by picking out their clothes or putting toys away. They can also do simple chores that help the whole family. What a good feeling it can be for them to know that it's not only adults who are the "helpers," but that children can be "helpers" too!

Feeling grownup

When children do grownup things, like setting a table, sorting laundry, or vacuuming the floor, they feel more grownup. In the long road toward independence, they need those small steps along the way to feel competent, capable, and more confident. What a good feeling it can be for children to know they're accomplishing something helpful and contributing in their own way to the family.

Working with you

We can't really expect young children to do too much on their own, especially when it comes to chores around the house. Because of safety reasons and because of preschoolers' own limited abilities, they need assistance from adults. As you work together, you will gain a "helper," and your child will gain that good feeling of working at your side. You might also learn more about your child in that time that you're spending together.

Do you know what else can happen when we adults use activities like the ones in this chapter to add a childhood sense of playful helpfulness to everyday household "chores?" We might just rediscover more of that child within us and see the playfulness carrying over to other so-called chores of our lives.

Laundry Matching

Any time that you're doing the laundry is a chance for sorting and matching games with your child.

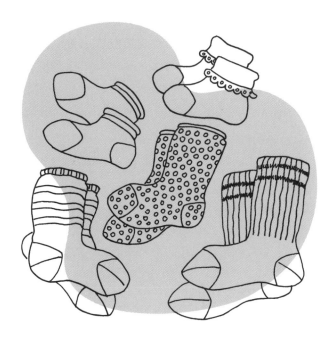

YOU'LL NEED:
Laundry to be sorted

* Show your child how you sort the laundry before putting it into the washer. Can your child sort into the piles of whites, darks, or bright colors? Things that are delicate or things that are sturdy?

* After the laundry is done, show your child that the clothes need to be sorted from each other again, but in different ways, when they're clean and it's time to put them away. For example, the white T-shirts or blue jeans need to be sorted according to size.

* Can your child pair up the socks?

* Ask your child to put each stack of clothing into the room where it belongs.

YOUR CHILD IS WORKING ON:
Responsibility
Classifying
Recognizing likeness and difference

As preschoolers are exposed to more things, people, and experiences, they try to make sense of the world by organizing things into categories. At this time in their lives, matching and sorting games can be especially appealing.

  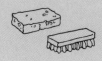

Clean-Up Magic

Here's a way to put some fun in clean-up time and to make it feel more manageable.

YOU'LL NEED:
Pieces of paper or index cards
Pencil or pen
Music from a tape or radio (optional)

✳ It's natural for young children to feel overwhelmed when they're asked to clean up their rooms. Sometimes a job feels more manageable when it is broken down into smaller specific tasks. Ask your child to help you come up with a list of things that need to be done to make the room clean. Here are some ideas:

> Pick up books
> Straighten the sheets and blanket
> Put dirty clothes in the laundry
> Put toys in their places

✳ Write each job on a separate piece of paper or on a separate index card.

✳ As if you're doing a magic trick, hold the papers (face down) fanned out like a deck of cards. You might even make a drum roll sound and ask your child to pick one card.

✳ Read the task aloud. For example, "Put the books on the bookshelf." Watch your child make the books "disappear" from the floor.

✳ When each task is done, ask your child to pick a new card. Pick a card for yourself, too.

✳ Another fun approach might be to turn on the radio, a tape, or CD and help your child put things away to the rhythm of the music.

YOUR CHILD IS WORKING ON:
Responsibility
Breaking down overwhelming tasks
  into smaller parts

> Children might worry that you will expect them to do all the work of cleaning up. If you work *with* your child, doing one chore while your child does another, the time will go faster, and you'll have some fun together.

    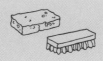

A Book of Coupon Gifts

Children can give help as well as receive it. Even young children have things they can do that are helpful in the family.

YOU'LL NEED:
Several sheets of paper
Blunt-nosed scissors
Markers or crayons
Stapler

* Start by cutting or tearing each piece of paper in half to make blank coupons.

* Ask your child to come up with ideas for ways that he or she can help the family. You or your child can write each idea on a coupon, or your child might want to draw a picture of each job. Here are some suggestions:

> Play quietly so a parent can have some peaceful time
> Give a hug
> Sort socks in the laundry
> Put out napkins for a meal

* Staple the coupons together, and let your child keep the coupon book. Then on special occasions, birthdays, holidays, or just any day, your child can give one of the coupons as a gift to someone in the family.

YOUR CHILD IS WORKING ON:
Responsibility
Literacy
Creativity

We give help, and we receive help, no matter how old or how young we are. As you work with your child to make coupons, you might want to make some of your own to give. In your own coupon book, you might include coupons for time with a parent, a treat at the ice cream store, or a backrub.

Washing Toys

Scrub-a-dub-dub! Turn a chore into irresistible water play.

YOU'LL NEED:

2 plastic dishpans
Water
Soap
Plastic tablecloth (optional)
Towels
Cloths or sponges
Old toothbrushes or scrub brushes
Washable toys

YOUR CHILD IS WORKING ON:
Responsibility
Independence

✻ Fill two dishpans with water. Add soap to one, and keep the other for rinsing. Set the dishpans on a plastic tablecloth or towel on the kitchen floor, bathtub, or sink. If the weather is warm, you could take the dishpans outdoors. Lay out a towel where the wet toys can be set to dry.

✻ Show your child how to wash his or her toys in the soapy water, and then how to rinse the toys in another dishpan.

✻ You may want to sing the children's folk song, "This is the way we wash our clothes . . ." Your child might want to make up other words to it. Here's an idea for the first verse:

> This is the way we wash our toys,
> Wash our toys, wash our toys.
> This is the way we wash our toys
> So early in the morning.

> Water play is like a magnet for many children. Maybe it's attractive because it doesn't put pressure on a child to "make something." Water play can even help children work on toilet training because they are learning to control their body fluids.

What's Your Job?

Turn everyday chores into a game of chance, and find fun in sharing the work.

YOU'LL NEED:
Large piece of paper or cardboard
Game spinner (see instructions on page 18)
Name tags
Tape

✳ On the paper or cardboard, list jobs everyone in the family can do and put the list where everyone can see it. Even a preschooler can help with some household chores, like:

> Sponge the table
> Put out napkins or spoons for a meal
> Water plants
> Pick up toys
> Help wash the car
> Sweep the rug

✳ Beside each job, write a number that corresponds to the numbers on a spinner.

✳ Take turns spinning the spinner to assign a job for the week to everyone in the family. Tape the corresponding name tag next to the chore on the chart.

✳ Remember that when you praise your children for being helpful, you are helping them feel proud of taking on responsibility.

YOUR CHILD IS WORKING ON:
Responsibility
Literacy
Number recognition

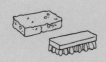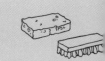

Milkshake Shake!

Milkshakes are usually made by machines, but they can also be made by hand. Let your child help and find a tasty reward at the end.

YOU'LL NEED:
1 quart plastic jar or container with
   a tight-fitting lid
Paper or plastic cups
Straws
Ingredients:
   ¾ scoop of ice cream (more if you want
      a thicker milkshake)
   1 cup of milk

Will make about 2 cups of milkshake.

✳ Scoop ice cream into a jar or plastic
   container. Add milk.

✳ Make sure the lid is on tightly, then let
   your child shake the container until the
   lumps of ice cream are dissolved.

✳ You can then pour the milkshake into cups
   and enjoy a treat that you've made together.

YOUR CHILD IS WORKING ON:
Appreciating the value of work
Awareness of science (how solids can change
   into liquids)
Measuring

When you're preparing a meal or snack, think about what parts of the work your child may be able to do. Being invited to be an "assistant chef" can make children feel proud, as well as more willing to try some new food they've helped prepare.

    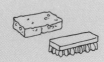

Playing Restaurant

Let your child help turn an ordinary meal into something special. Here's a great idea for leftover night or when your child invites a friend over for a meal.

YOU'LL NEED:
Menus made on paper
Pad and pencil
Chef hat (see page 35)
Tray
Play money or pretend credit cards

* Decide what food to serve, then work with the children to write the menus. If you have a young child, you'll probably have to do the writing, or your child can draw pictures for the different foods.

* Talk with the children about jobs in the restaurant. Ask them to choose a position. Someone might have to double up on duties, just like in some real restaurants. The positions can be:

> Waiter/waitress (hand out menus, take food orders)
> Busboy/girl (set the table, clear the table after the meal)
> Chef (cook the food)
> Cashier (take money, make change)

* While you're giving the children a fun way to be involved with getting the meal ready and cleaning up, you're also giving them the opportunity to try different roles and see things from a different perspective.

YOUR CHILD IS WORKING ON:
Responsibility
Cooperation
Dramatic play
Literacy
Imagination

> **If you've written the words for the menu, your child is reading even if he or she knows only the first letter of the word. "Reading" pictures on a menu is also a beginning step towards reading words.**

Neighborhood Helpers

Helping isn't just something we do at home. There are lots of people who do important jobs that help a whole neighborhood or town.

YOU'LL NEED:
Magazines or newspapers
Blunt-nosed scissors
Paste
Blank paper
Stapler

* Have your child look through some magazines and/or newspapers and ask him or her to find pictures of community helpers, like:

> Office worker
> Mail carrier
> Truck driver
> Doctor, dentist, nurse
> Teacher
> Waitress, waiter, or chef

* Paste the pictures onto the blank paper and write the names of the jobs next to the pictures.

* Staple the pages together, and you've made a book.

YOUR CHILD IS WORKING ON:
Appreciating people who help
Learning about different jobs
Literacy
Dexterity

> When children know that everyone's job is important, they gain an appreciation for people and value all kinds of work. They can also feel more secure knowing that many people help take care of them and their family.

Things that Go

Making playthings

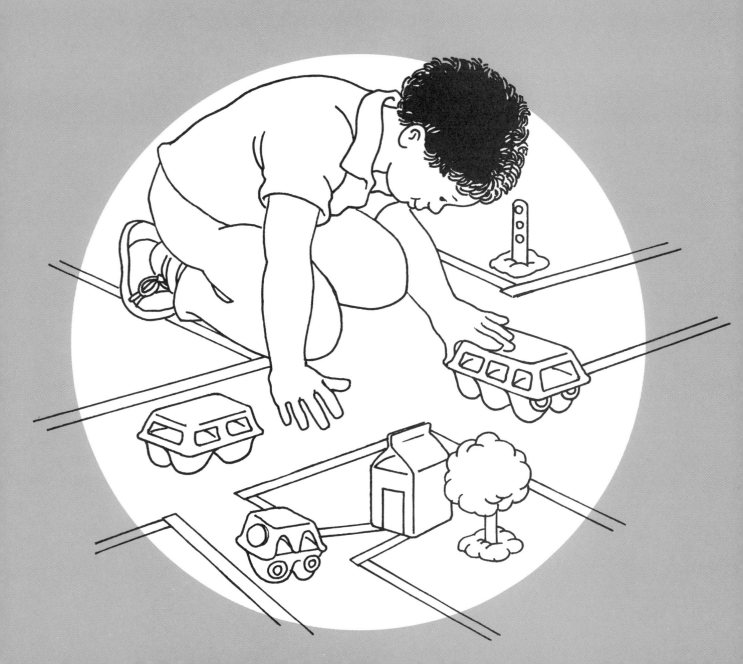

A friend of mine has a three-year-old son who is fascinated with trucks. "Trucks! That's all David talks about day and night!" his mother told me. "When we're looking at a book, he's interested only if there's a truck on the page, even if it's just a tiny toy on a shelf in the background. At bedtime, he won't go to sleep until he's recited a list of all the trucks he saw that day. It seems like trucks are all he thinks about."

Delighting in movement

Boys and girls can be fascinated by all sorts of things that move. An attraction to cars, trucks, buses, and trains usually begins at the same time children start crawling or walking. They're so intensely involved in learning how to get around that they can be captivated by anything suggesting movement, or anything they can move smoothly along the floor or table top.

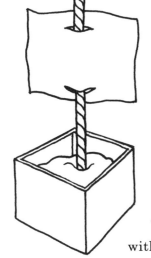

Many vehicles go fast, whether they're on wheels, in the air, or on water—and they move with such ease! What a delight they are to play with, especially for children who are just learning to walk and run—or who have recently done a lot of falling and getting back up and trying again!

Feeling powerful

Powerful vehicles like trains, trucks, and construction vehicles can become fascinating to children as they come to recognize that, instead of being at the center of the universe, they're not in charge of much at all. They don't have control over when to eat, how long they stay at the playground, or when they go to bed—someone else makes those decisions. Children can find real comfort in being in charge of playthings that are symbols of power—like trucks, cars, buses, trains, planes, bulldozers, and backhoes.

Developing self-control

With all their speed, vehicles have to be driven with caution—trains and trolleys need tracks, cars and buses need to stay on the road. When children play with toy vehicles, they can work on their own inner controls—their growing ability to stop and start and stay on track. Making a toy car stop can be a fun way to play about self-control. I've seen children "lock" their cars in toy garages (made from a cardboard box), maybe a symbolic move to keep their own negative urges locked up tight!

Dealing with feelings

When children are angry or frustrated or disappointed, you might find them crashing their trucks and cars into each other. While this looks like violent play and can make some adults uncomfortable, it can be a healthy way to express aggression on inanimate objects instead of people.

Coming and going

I know a girl who used a toy car to help whenever she felt lonely or sad. She would run the car up her arms, all the way up to the top of her head, saying, "Bye-bye. I'm goin' away." Then she'd roll it back down again, saying, "Going home now."

Playing with vehicles that take people away and bring them back is a way of giving expression to children's fears of being separated from people they love. Making toy cars, trucks, boats, and planes go away and come back again gives children a chance to work through some of their feelings about separation and return. What's more, in their play, they're in charge of who goes away, who comes back, and when! Cars, boats, and planes can indeed be "vehicles" for lots of healthy growth.

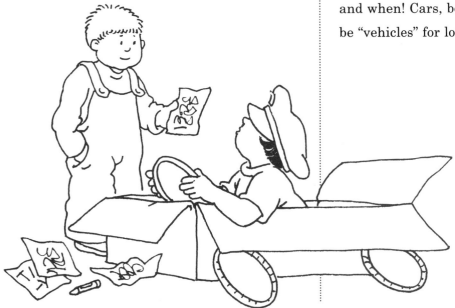

Egg Carton Cars

Turn an empty egg carton into a car to zoom around the room.

YOU'LL NEED:

Blunt-nosed scissors

Styrofoam or cardboard egg carton

Garbage bag twist ties

Glue

Marker

Cardboard box (optional for garage)

Plastic wrap (optional)

✳ Start by cutting off the end of an egg carton so that there are four egg spaces for the wheels on the car. There will be a hinge on one side so that the top can swing open and shut.

✳ Next, cut the side and back panels to make windows. Your child may want to use plastic wrap for windows and windshields.

✳ Add a safety message by including seatbelts in the car. Poke slits in the sides of the passenger wells and thread twist ties through the carton where the seats are.

✳ With another twist tie, make a door latch to keep the top shut.

✳ Use a thick magic marker to draw shapes that look like headlights on the front, brake lights on the back, and spoked wheels on the sides.

✳ A cardboard box can easily become a garage.

YOUR CHILD IS WORKING ON:

Following directions

Pretending

Dexterity

Imagination

Merrily We Roll Along

What things can roll? Wheels, marbles, balls? Children can, too!

YOU'LL NEED:
Blanket (optional)
Hillside outdoors (optional)

* Children can roll safely if they lie on the floor with their hands folded across their chests and roll over to the other end of a blanket or up to some piece of furniture across the room.

* If it's a warm, dry day, your child may want to use this technique for rolling down a hill.

YOUR CHILD IS WORKING ON:
Coordination
Observation of physical principles

While some children love the sensation and freedom of rolling down a little hill, other children may not like it. They may want to roll something else, like a toy car, down the hill.

Keeping on Track

Draw tracks and streets on an ordinary paper bag or old sheet, and you've got a place to play with toy vehicles—and a place to practice staying in-bounds. Keeping toy trolleys on the track or cars on the road can help children practice self-control.

YOU'LL NEED:
Several large grocery bags or an old bed sheet
Masking tape
Markers
Toy cars or homemade versions
Blocks or boxes for toy trolleys or buses

* To make a large mat for trolley or toy car play, tape several large grocery bags together or spread an old sheet on the floor. Draw a set of trolley tracks or roads on the mat with a marker, or put masking tape on the floor for tracks or roads. Older children may want to make their own tracks or roads.

* Have your child drive the toy cars or trolleys on the roads or tracks. Remind your child to keep the cars and trolleys within the boundaries of the roads and tracks just like people do when they drive real cars and trolleys.

YOUR CHILD IS WORKING ON:
Self-control
Coordination
Pretending

This can be a helpful activity when children are struggling with following rules at home, childcare, preschool, or school. This activity is also a fun way for children to use their fingers carefully to stay in the lines, an important skill for learning to write.

Building a Neighborhood

You and your child might enjoy building a whole neighborhood around the roads and tracks you create in the activity on the previous page. Here are some easy playthings to make to fill in the community.

* **Buildings:** Use milk cartons or cereal boxes covered with construction paper to create buildings. Add windows and doors by drawing or pasting squares of paper.

* **Tunnels and Bridges:** Cut cardboard oatmeal canisters in half lengthwise and set them on the ground to make tunnels for toy cars to go through. Blocks and cardboard boxes can also make bridges.

* **Traffic lights:** Paste three circles (red, yellow, and green) on each of several popsicle sticks. Put the sticks in clay bases to keep them steady (see page 92).

* **Stop signs:** Cut a piece of cardboard into several octagons and write the word STOP on them. Glue the cardboard octagons onto popsicle sticks and put them into play clay bases at the intersections.

* **Fire hydrants:** Paint corks red and glue them in the sidewalk area.

* **Mail box:** Stand a large-size kitchen match box on its end. Leave the drawer open a half inch or so at the top, and your child can drop "letters" in.

* **Shrubs:** Cotton balls painted green make good shrubs, particularly if you tug gently on the cotton to stretch it out and then spread it into clumps. Put shrubs into clay bases (see page 92).

YOUR CHILD IS WORKING ON:
Creativity
Dexterity
Imagination
Resourcefulness (finding new uses for things)

All Aboard!

Add some imagination to your kitchen chairs, and you've got all the ingredients you need for a pretend trip!

YOU'LL NEED:
Chairs
Construction paper "tickets"
Belts

✳ Let your child line up chairs in pairs or in rows. Friends or family members can pretend to buy "tickets" (imaginary tickets or tickets made from construction paper) to get a ride.

✳ Be sure to fasten your seat belts by putting a belt behind the chair and bringing it around to the front.

✳ If you're one of the passengers, you could pretend to look out the window and talk about what you see. You can stimulate your child's imagination by saying something like, "Look, there's a big truck next to us. What do you think is inside it?" or "That woman is all dressed up. Where do you think she's going?"

YOUR CHILD IS WORKING ON:
Playing about power and control
Coping with separation and return
Pretending
Imagination

> Children often feel left behind when their favorite grownups go off in cars and planes. Before you go away, or after you come back, your child may want to use this pretend play to be in charge of who gets a ticket and who has to stay behind.

A Sailboat

Any kind of water play is a natural attraction for many children.

YOU'LL NEED:
Blunt-nosed scissors
Waxed milk cartons (pint or quart size)
Lightweight paper
Straw or stick
Modeling dough or play clay (see page 92)
Sink, bathtub, dishpan, or outdoor wading
    pool with water

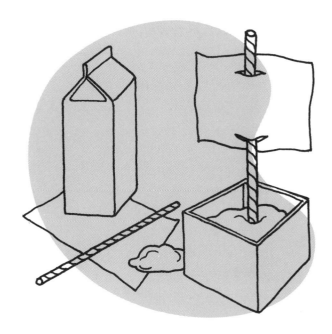

* For the body of the boat, cut the milk carton from the base so that the carton has a bottom and is about 3" tall.

* Fasten the paper to a stick or straw to make a sail, then set it in place by sticking it into a piece of clay or modeling dough in the bottom of the milk carton.

* Now your boat is ready for its maiden voyage. Show your child how to blow on the sail, and watch how the boat moves through the water. You might want to talk with your child about real sailboats and what makes them move.

YOUR CHILD IS WORKING ON:
Awareness of science (learning about
    physical principles of wind)
Learning about cause and effect
Self-control

Children soon learn that the boat will tip over if it they blow on it too hard, so they have to use some self-control in blowing.

A Balloon Boat

Here's a "power" boat—powered by the air in a balloon!

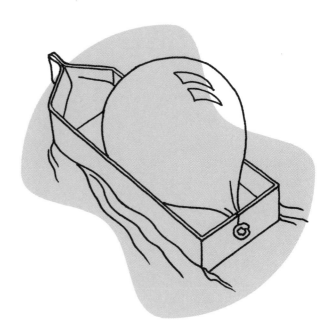

YOU'LL NEED:
Waxed milk carton (quart size)
Blunt-nosed scissors
Balloon

* Lay a waxed milk carton on its side with the opened spout facing upwards. Cut it in half, lengthwise, to make a sturdy hull for a boat from the half without the open spout.

* Poke a small hole in the back wall of the boat. The size of the hole will determine how fast the boat will go and how long the boat will glide across the water.

* Cut a thin slit down to the hole from the top.

* Blow up a balloon, and stretch it at the mouthpiece. Work it down the slit to the hole in the back wall, with the balloon inside of the milk carton.

* Keep the opening of the balloon pinched shut on the outside of the boat. When you're ready, let go.

* If you'd like, you and your child can try several variations of this activity, using different sized cartons, or altering the size of the hole in the back of the boat. Can your child figure out which variations go faster or longer? By experimenting, you may end up with a craft that moves really well.

YOUR CHILD IS WORKING ON:
Awareness of science (learning about the physical principles of air)
Learning about cause and effect
Dexterity

A Banana Boat

Most recipes require cooking or cutting or adult supervision. This is one of the few snacks children can make in the kitchen all by themselves.

YOU'LL NEED:
Slice of bread
Peanut butter
½ banana
2 thin pretzel sticks

* Spread the peanut butter on the slice of bread.

* Place the half of a banana on the bread.

* Fold the bread in half to make a "boat."

* Insert two thin pretzel sticks into the sides, like oars, to hold the bread together.

YOUR CHILD IS WORKING ON:
Dexterity
Pretending
Making healthy food choices

Row, Row, Row Your Boat

Here's a familiar song to use for exercise and muscle control, and it gives your child a way to have fun with words.

YOU'LL NEED:
Chair, blanket, or rug

✳ Show your child the arm motions for rowing. You could sit in a chair or on a blanket or rug on the floor and pretend to be rowing while you sing the song "Row, Row, Row Your Boat."

✳ For variation, sing and row slowly at first, then faster each time, then slower and slower.

✳ After you sing the original words for this song, you and your child might like to sing a royal version, sung to the same melody by King Friday XIII (ruler of the Neighborhood of Make-Believe on *Mister Rogers' Neighborhood*):

"Propel, Propel, Propel Your Craft"

Propel, propel, propel your craft
Gently down liquid solution.
Ecstatically, ecstatically,
Ecstatically, ecstatically,
Existence is but an illusion.

YOUR CHILD IS WORKING ON:
Coordination
Rhythm
Self-control
Language development

Once children have mastered a language, they often want to "play" with that language by using big words or even made-up words. You might want to use those new fancy words in everyday conversation with your child, asking him or her, "Would you like a glass of liquid solution?" or "I'm ecstatic over what you've just made."

Parachute Play

Flying or floating playthings move so effortlessly through the air. No wonder children are fascinated by them.

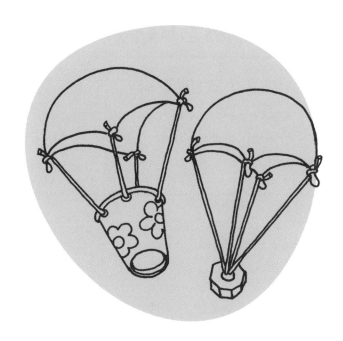

YOU'LL NEED:
Handkerchief or square piece of cloth
String (4" or 8" pieces for each parachute)
Small paper cups or metal nut/washer
Pencil

✱ To make a parachute, knot an 8-inch piece of string to each corner of a handkerchief or piece of cloth.

✱ Using a pencil, poke 4 holes around the rim of a paper cup and fasten the end of each string to the holes. For a different kind of parachute, tie the ends of the strings to a metal nut or washer, instead of using a cup.

✱ Your child can put toy people or small animals inside the cups—they'll add the necessary weight to make the parachutes float properly.

✱ Toss the parachute in the air, and watch it open and float to the ground.

YOUR CHILD IS WORKING ON:
Awareness of science (learning about movement of things in the air)
Following directions
Pretending

Memory Game

Bring out some of your child's playthings for this memory game to exercise your child's mind. Play and learning go hand in hand, in many ways!

YOU'LL NEED:
Toy cars or other toy vehicles
Table top or towel

* Put 3 to 5 (depending on your child's memory level) of your child's toy vehicles on a table or on a towel. Your child might have an easier time remembering the toys if you describe them as you put them on the table.

* Give your child some time to look carefully at the toys.

* Ask your child to turn his or her back, and take away one toy.

* When you're ready, ask your child to turn back around and tell you which toy is missing.

* If your child can't remember which toy is missing, ask him or her to look away again while you put that toy back in the line-up. Then ask him or her to identify which toy you put back.

* You and your child could take turns being the one who chooses the toy and the one who guesses.

YOUR CHILD IS WORKING ON:
Memory
Observation skills

Away We Go!

A cardboard box can be the start of lots of imaginative play—let your child sit in it, and watch his or her pretend play take flight.

YOU'LL NEED:
Cardboard box big enough for your child
   to sit in
Construction paper
Tape
Markers
Pie pan (optional for steering wheel)
Tin foil (optional)

✽ A box can become an airplane if you tape wings on it. You might want to help your child draw gauges on the inside front.

✽ To become a car, all the box needs are shiny headlights (from pie pans or tin foil and a steering wheel made from a pie pan or paper circle).

✽ With broom sticks or yard sticks for oars, the box turns into a boat!

✽ If you feel your child needs some help getting involved in this kind of play, try asking questions like:

> Where are you going?
> Who will be there?
> What will you see there?

YOUR CHILD IS WORKING ON:
Dramatic play
Creativity
Pretending

Feelings

Finding ways to express
all kinds of feelings

When I see children making angry paintings, dancing happy dances, composing sad songs, or taming scary puppets, I see childhood at its healthiest, for those are children's ways of expressing feelings.

Early on in my life, I found an outlet that worked well for me. When I was four years old, my parents told me I could choose what I wanted for my birthday from a toy catalog. When I saw the toy piano on one of the pages, that was it! Maybe I was drawn to music because I saw how much my grandfather enjoyed playing the violin, or maybe because I heard the pleasure that my parents and grandparents had in singing lullabies and listening to music.

Music soon became my way to express who I am. When I was angry as a child, my family wouldn't allow me to crash and stomp around through the house, but they did encourage me to play out my feelings on the piano. That's when I discovered the real power of music. I'd begin by banging random notes—anything, almost like punching at the keys. The longer I played, though, the calmer my music became, and the calmer I became, too. That piano probably got me out of a lot of trouble! To this day, I can still laugh and cry and express my anger through the tips of my fingers on piano keys.

Feelings are a part of being human, and when we encourage children to talk and play about their feelings, we are helping them find constructive ways of expressing their true selves—ways that won't hurt them or anyone else.

Talking about feelings

Whatever is mentionable can be more manageable, but young children often have trouble telling us what they're feeling. Many of them don't use words well yet. Sometimes feelings are a jumble inside and hard to sort out or to name. Through play, we can encourage children to put their feelings into words.

Being able to use words to describe what they're feeling gives children power over their feelings. Giving words to feelings can make them become a lot less overwhelming or upsetting or scary. Also, when children can talk about their feelings with a caring listener, they find out that their feelings are natural and normal, and that others have felt that way, too.

Developing inner controls

Self-control grows little by little and over a long time. Some of the activities in this section will allow your child to practice self-control to stop from hurting someone and to experience the good feeling of being in control of their actions.

Finding outlets for feelings

Have you noticed that you get tense and tight when you're upset, angry, or worried? There's a lot of physical energy tied up in feelings. When children have healthy outlets, they have ways to release some of the energy that is bound up inside.

What works as a release for one child may not work for another. It can take a while until a child finds some way of expression that's comfortable for him or her. That's why we've offered lots of different activities—music, painting, working with clay, physical activity—so that children can discover what feels right for them.

Go-Stop-Go

Combine music with this "freeze" game to give your child a jazzy way to practice self-control.

YOU'LL NEED:
Music on the radio or tape

* Find some music on the radio or tape that's good for marching or other kind of spirited dancing.

* Tell your child to listen for the music—to march or dance when it's on and to stop moving when the music stops. (This works best if you can turn your back so your child can't see when you stop the music.)

* When your child manages to stop, you have a wonderful opportunity to say something like, "See, you can control yourself! Good job!"

* Remember, it's hard to calm down after doing a lively activity, so it's a good idea to play softer, slower music to help your child wind down gradually.

YOUR CHILD IS WORKING ON:
Self-control
Listening skills
Coordination

Most children have trouble stopping in mid-air in the middle of a musical beat. It's even harder for them to control their hands from hitting when they're angry. Over time, your child will probably get better at this musical game, and that growing ability can extend to other times when your child needs self-control. When you notice the progress, let your child know you're proud of him or her. On our *Neighborhood* programs, we call that "inside growing."

Rice Cake Faces

Round rice cakes make a great base for a face that can show different emotions and generate some healthy talk about feelings.

YOU'LL NEED:
Rice cakes
Spreading knife
Peanut butter or cream cheese
Raisins
Apple slices
Bananas

✻ Let your child spread a rice cake with peanut butter or cream cheese. That's the foundation for a face.

✻ What kind of feeling would your child would like to make on the rice cake face? Raisins could be used for eyes, noses, or mouths. An apple slice can make a smiling or frowning mouth. A banana chunk could be a nose. A banana slice could be a surprised mouth or eyes.

✻ You may want to ask your child to talk about what makes him or her feel angry, sad, surprised, scared, or happy.

YOUR CHILD IS WORKING ON:
Naming feelings
Talking about feelings
Imagination
Dexterity
Making healthy food choices

A Doll as Big as Me!

Help your child make a life-sized doll—and work on an important life skill: self-control that begins with being aware of body boundaries.

YOU'LL NEED:
20 or more sheets of newspaper
Blunt-nosed scissors
Tape
Stapler
Marker or paint and brushes

✻ On the floor, tape two or three sheets of newspaper together to make an area that's large enough for your child to lie on. Make three more layers of the same size.

✻ Have your child lie down on the four layers of paper, then trace the outline of your child's body, from head to toe.

✻ Cut around the outline through all four layers. Staple or tape the four layers around the edges, leaving one side open.

✻ Gently stuff the outline with more sheets of crumpled newspaper. Leave two layers of paper on either side of the stuffing so the doll won't tear so easily. When the outline has been stuffed, staple or tape shut the open side.

✻ Your child might want to draw or paint features and clothes on the doll.

YOUR CHILD IS WORKING ON:
Self-control (through an awareness of body boundaries)
Pretending
Imagination

As you draw around your child's hands and feet, your child is having physical sensations that reinforce where his or her hands and legs end. In order for children to be able to control their hands and feet when they're angry (so they don't hurt anyone), they first need to have that clear sense of where their hands and feet end.

Wheel of Feelings

Encourage helpful talk about feelings with this activity.

YOU'LL NEED:
Spinner (see instructions on page 18)
Marker
Magazine or newspaper pictures (optional)

* Make a spinner. Instead of using numbers, your child can draw a face showing a different feeling on each section, or your child could paste a picture of a person showing a different feeling on each segment. The spinner can include :

> Anger
> Sadness
> Surprise
> Happiness
> Fear

* Ask your child to spin the spinner, and pretend to show the emotion where the spinner stops with his or her face, body, hands, legs, and voice. You could expand this by asking your child to make up a story about someone who feels that way.

* If you keep the spinner handy, your child could use it to show how he or she is feeling any day.

YOUR CHILD IS WORKING ON:
Naming feelings
Talking about feelings

It may help to remind your child that while we may know some things about how people feel by looking at their faces, the only way we can *really* know how they feel is if they tell us. No one can know exactly what we're thinking or feeling unless we tell them.

A Festival of Mad Feelings

This could be an activity for a day when your child has had a disappointment—like when a trip is canceled or when a friend can't come to play. Turn the disappointment into an occasion to give your child ways of expressing angry feelings.

YOU'LL NEED:
Play clay (see recipe on page 92)
Pillows
Drums or pots and pans
Crunchy foods like celery, apple chunks,
   or carrot sticks

✳ Before you start the Festival of Mad Feelings, give your child some rules, like:

> Play clay is to be kept on the table.
> Pound only the pillows, play clay, or drums—not people.
> When I give a signal to stop, you need to stop.

✳ It would be a good idea to begin with short time limits for pounding (15 or 30 seconds) to make sure your child can stop. Then increase to a minute or two of pounding.

✳ You could also set up areas for throwing pillows, for making a mad picture, or for making up a mad dance or song.

✳ For the grand finale, offer a snack of crunchy celery, apple, or carrot sticks for teeth chomping.

YOUR CHILD IS WORKING ON:
Finding healthy outlets for anger
Self-control

> **We can help children know it's okay to be angry but it's not okay to hurt. Through activities like these we can encourage them to find constructive ways to express those feelings.**

"Get Out the Mad" Cookies

These cookies taste better the more your child pounds on the dough.

YOU'LL NEED:
Large bowl
Cookie sheet
Oven preheated to 350°F
Ingredients:

    3 cups oatmeal
    1½ cups brown sugar
    1½ cups all-purpose flour
    1½ cups butter or margarine
    1½ teaspoons baking powder

✳ Place all the ingredients in a large bowl, and mix them well.

✳ Give your child a manageable chunk of dough. It's okay for your child to mash it, knead it, and pound it. The longer and harder your child mixes the dough, the better the cookies taste!

✳ When the mixing is done, show your child how to roll the dough into balls about the size of ping-pong balls, and place them on the cookie sheet.

✳ Bake the cookies 350°F for 10 to 12 minutes.

YOUR CHILD IS WORKING ON:
Finding healthy outlets for anger
Following directions
Literacy
Measuring
Patience

> **Following recipes involves reading and following directions. Your child can see firsthand how helpful it is to be able to read numbers and to measure carefully.**

Taming a Scary Puppet

By creating a scary puppet and then taming it, your child may learn to tame other scary things in his or her life.

YOU'LL NEED:
Paper bag
Construction paper
Blunt-nosed scissors
Yarn
Glue

✳ A paper bag is all you need to start making a puppet. Talk with your child about what would make the puppet look scary. Have your child paste eyes, a nose, ears, a mouth, and teeth on the puppet. Use yarn for hair or for a beard.

✳ While your child is making the puppet, you could talk about things that are scary for your child—like an animal's big teeth or loud sounds.

✳ When the puppet is finished, let your child talk with the puppet and find ways to "tame" it so it isn't so scary. You might suggest that the puppet is scary because it's sad or mad about something, helping your child to make up a story about the puppet's concerns.

YOUR CHILD IS WORKING ON:
Using play to work on fears
Talking about feelings
Creativity
Pretending

> Some families find puppets to be helpful for children who have had nightmares or other scary experiences. But for some children, even a scary puppet is too frightening. If this is the case, you may be able to help your child make up stories about someone or an animal who was scared.

Note: For more on puppet play, see pages 38–42.

Not-So-Scary Shadows

Shadows can seem scary at night when children don't understand what they are. Turn them into playful fun in the daytime, and a way to offer some reassuring talk about other things that may be scary for your child.

YOU'LL NEED:
Bright light (such as a desk lamp or flashlight)

✳ Shine the light on the wall. Have your child stand between the light and the wall.

✳ Show your child how to use his or her hands, fingers, or body to make shadows. You may want to take turns making shadows and guessing what the shape is.

✳ You might use these or some of your own:

> Make a deer by putting your thumb and forefinger together, with other fingers up for the antlers.
>
> Make a rabbit by holding down your last two fingers with your thumb and putting your forefinger and middle finger up for the ears.
>
> Make a dog or alligator with a big mouth by keeping the back of your palms together and moving your hands like a hinge.

YOUR CHILD IS WORKING ON:
Using play to work on fears
Talking about feelings
Pretending

Doctor Play

Playing about a visit to the doctor gives your child a way to rehearse some procedures that may happen there—to be the one in charge of doing the examination and giving the injection.

YOU'LL NEED:

Smock or old white shirt

A doctor's bag with some of the following:

   Tongue depressors

   Strips of cloth bandages

   Yardstick or tape measure
     (to measure height)

   Ballpoint pen without the ink
     cartridge (for pretend injections)

   Lightweight radio headphones with
     the wires hanging from them or
     an empty spool strung on a yarn
     (for a stethoscope)

   Plastic bubble wand (for checking eyes
     and ears)

* Doctor play is so inviting that it usually doesn't need much introduction. Many children like to examine their stuffed animals or dolls. Or you may want to pretend to be the patient.

YOUR CHILD IS WORKING ON:

Using play to work on fears

Role-playing

Pretending

Playing about experiences that might be upsetting or scary can help your child feel less helpless—and trust you more because of your honest and reassuring help beforehand.

A Softee Friend

A soft cuddly stuffed "friend" can be comforting for your child to hold.

YOU'LL NEED:
Pillowcase (large or small)
Stuffing for the pillowcase—old rags, dryer lint, cotton batting, and/or foam rubber
Yarn
Buttons (optional)
Fabric scraps

✳ Stuff the pillowcase and tie it shut at the top with colorful yarn.

✳ Tie another piece of yarn around the middle for a waist or neck.

✳ Tie two pieces of yarn around the bottom corners to make feet.

✳ To make a face, you might use circles, triangles, or crescents of fabric for eyes, eyebrows, nose, and mouth. Does your child want the "softee friend" to look happy or neutral or sad or angry? Maybe your child wants to have two different expressions— one on each side of the pillowcase.

YOUR CHILD IS WORKING ON:
Using play to work on fears
Pretending

Sometimes a bit of comfort is all a child needs in order to refuel before feeling ready to move on. Just knowing you helped make this "softee" can give it even more value at a lonely or sad time.

A Sign of Growing

Here's a way to give your child the good feeling of pride for the small and big steps of growing inside and out.

YOU'LL NEED:
Paper (enough to make an approximately 11"x17" sign)
Pen or marker

✱ Tape the paper horizontally on the wall with the top of the paper at your child's height.

✱ Most growing charts show how much children grow outside. It's just as important for children to feel good about how much they're growing inside. On this one, you could note and date events, like:

> shared with a friend
> waited for a turn
> caught a ball
> used the potty
> cut with scissors
> said "I'm mad" instead of hitting
> rode a tricycle
> dressed without help
> wrote my name
> tied my own shoelaces

✱ If you make a new growing sign each month, you'll have a scrapbook of the many ways your child is growing.

YOUR CHILD IS WORKING ON:
Feelings of pride
Patience
Literacy

We all seem to make a fuss at the big moments of growing, like birthdays and first days at school, but what a good feeling it can be for your child to know you're proud of him or her at the little moments. Look for those moments to celebrate, like when your child is about to hit someone but stops. What an important time to say "I'm really proud of you." That's a great moment of self-control—a great moment to celebrate!

Creative Fun

Encouraging self-expression

One day in our office, we received a large envelope from Dallas, Texas. The letter, attached to eleven pieces of music paper, started out by saying: "Enclosed please find an opera, no less, written by a six-year-old viewer who was inspired by your programs." And there it was: a little boy's opera about an owl and a tiger and a king and an archaeologist who discover that what others thought was a monster was just a blinking flashlight caught in a tunnel. An opera by a six year old! Of course, his mother had written the words and the notes on the music paper for him and the characters are those he visits via our program every day—but the opera is his. He wanted to make one and someone encouraged him to try.

Most children don't write operas; nevertheless, every child is born with a unique endowment which gives him or her an opportunity to make something entirely different from everybody else in the world. You see it when you watch children at their own play. No two mud pies are the same. Block buildings have infinite variety. Paintings and dances take on their creators' touches, and later, hairstyles, jewelry, and language reflect individuality. When you see it all happening, you know something from inside is being shared with the rest of the world.

Each person has something no one else has or will ever have. Encouraging our children to discover their uniqueness and helping develop its creative expression can be one of the greatest gifts and one of the greatest delights of parenthood.

Creative materials

Hand children some raw materials, and they'll find their own ways to use them. You probably have lots of these materials around the house—maybe they're even throw-aways, like paper towel tubes, egg cartons, buttons, popsicle sticks, or shoe boxes. You might say, "Here's an empty box, what can you make from it?"

Having crayons, markers, construction paper, tape, or glue accessible can turn "What can I do?" times into "Look what I made!" times.

Responding to children's creativity

Because children need to know they're loved by the people they care about most, our interest and approval can play a big part in encouraging their developing creativity. But sometimes in our wanting to give encouragement, our enthusiasm can be counter-productive. Suppose Carla is angry at her brother. As she's painting her feelings of anger on the easel with large messy strokes of paint, an adult comes over and says, "That's very nice, Carla." Well, Carla might not mean it to be nice at all. She may mean it to be messy and ugly and "mad"—just the way she's feeling.

What's the best adult response? Quiet looking and listening—waiting for the moment when Carla might let you know what she wants you to know. There is so often much more than meets the eye! (And how much better that Carla could let her anger out on the easel rather than by hurting someone or ruining something.)

Process is more important than product

There can also be much less than meets the eye, as with young toddlers and preschoolers who are generally more fascinated by the process than by the product. When they paint, they marvel at how the paint drips down the papers. "Let me make whatever happens" they seem to be saying. It's much safer for adults to say, "Would you like to tell me about it?" than to ask, "What is it?" Children might say, "Nothing" or make up elaborate stories about their "drips." Either way, it's their "creation" to describe if they're so inspired!

We don't have to understand all of a child's creative efforts. What's important is that we communicate our respect for their attempts to express what's inside themselves. It's the creating that we need to encourage.

Stained Glass Windows

You'll probably find bits of crayon pieces in your child's crayon box. Instead of throwing them out, show your child a new use for them in these colorful window hangings.

Wax Paper

YOU'LL NEED:

Crayon sharpener or plastic knife
Old crayon pieces
Cardboard or sturdy portable surface
2 pieces of wax paper, approximately
   the same size
Iron

* With a crayon sharpener or plastic knife, shave off slivers of crayon onto a piece of wax paper placed on top of a larger piece of cardboard or other sturdy, portable surface.

* Let your child arrange the shavings on the wax paper, then cover them with another piece of wax paper.

* Carefully transfer the wax paper to an ironing board. Use a thin dishtowel between the wax paper and the iron.

* Press the sheets of wax paper together with a warm iron. The crayon shavings will melt and run together, making interesting designs. Don't let the iron get too hot—the wax will burn, ruining the colors and causing an unpleasant odor.

* After the wax dries, hang the design in the window and watch the light shine through it, just like through a stained glass window.

YOUR CHILD IS WORKING ON:

Creativity
Awareness of science (learning about
   effect of heat)
Dexterity

Colorful Containers

Here's a great way to reuse an empty can! Before you begin, make sure that the can you're using doesn't have a sharp edge that could cut little fingers.

YOU'LL NEED:
Empty can (i.e. from coffee, soup, yogurt, or frozen juice)
Cotton swab or small brush
Glue
Any or all of the following: yarn, construction paper, scraps of felt, tissue paper, magazine pictures

✱ Give your child a cotton swab or small brush to cover the sides of the can with glue.

✱ Let your child decorate the can however he or she likes. Your child might wrap yarn in coils all the way around the container, or add construction paper, fabric or felt scraps, bits of paper, or magazine pictures.

✱ When the glue has dried, your child might use the cup as a container for pencils, crayons, or toys, or give it as a gift to someone.

YOUR CHILD IS WORKING ON:
Creativity
Dexterity
Resourcefulness (finding new uses for old things)

Paper Mobiles

Paper mobiles are fun to make and fun to watch as they move in the air.

YOU'LL NEED:
Construction paper in different colors
Blunt-nosed scissors
Paper punch or sharp pencil
String
Coat hangers or wooden dowels
Crayons
Glue or paste

✻ Have your child cut or tear pieces of the colored paper into shapes or glue several shapes together, one on top of the other, for a 3D effect.

✻ Poke or punch a hole at the top of each shape.

✻ Tie a piece of string through the hole and fasten the other end to the coat hanger or dowel.

✻ Cut the string at various lengths to make a more interesting mobile.

YOUR CHILD IS WORKING ON:
Creativity
Awareness of science (learning about movement of things in the air)

Making a Book

Your child can be author and illustrator—and bookbinder!

YOU'LL NEED:

Cardboard (from the backs of tablets or
    empty cereal boxes)
Blunt-nosed scissors
Paper for pages (heavier paper works best)
Fabric
Glue
Paper punch
Yarn, shoelaces, heavy string, or
    notebook rings
Old magazines or catalogs
Crayons, markers, or colored pencils

* Make front and back covers by cutting two
  pieces of cardboard a little larger than the
  paper pages you'll be using. Your child can
  glue fabric to make fancy covers.

* Put 5 or 6 pages between the covers, punch
  holes along one side, and let your child lace
  the pages together with yarn.

* Let your child cut and paste magazine
  pictures on the pages. Maybe your child
  wants to draw pictures or make up a poem
  or song for you to write in the book.

* You may want to suggest a theme for
  the book or for certain pages, like animal
  pictures, my favorite things, alphabet
  pictures, or families.

YOUR CHILD IS WORKING ON:
Imagination
Decision-making
Dexterity
Literacy

> **Imagine how exciting it can be for
> your child to "read" a book he or
> she has made. Even naming things
> in pictures can be an important step
> for reading readiness.**

Mix a Batch of Play Clay

Here are some easy, economical ways to make your own clay for all kinds of creative play.

PLAY CLAY #1

1 cup flour
½ cup salt
2 teaspoons cream of tartar
1 cup water
A few drops food coloring (optional)
1 tablespoon oil

* Mix the flour, salt, and cream of tartar in a small bowl.

* In a separate bowl, mix the liquids. Use the food coloring to mix your own colors.

* Combine the two mixtures and cook on medium to low heat, stirring until the combination is the consistency of mashed potatoes.

* When the mixture is cool, knead it a little. Store in a covered container.

PLAY CLAY #2

2 cups flour
1 cup salt
1 cup water
1 teaspoon salad oil (optional)

* Combine and mix all ingredients and store in an air-tight container.

* Keep in mind that toddlers might be tempted to eat the clay, so if there's a chance they may be around, it may be better to lower the salt content.

YOUR CHILD IS WORKING ON:
Following directions
Coordination
Creativity

Found Object Sculpture

Search your toolbox and catch-all drawers for raw materials to recycle for this activity.

Children are fascinated with the feel of different textures and the look of different shapes. That's why "junk" drawers, with their bits and pieces of hardware items and other things, are full of treasures for this kind of creative play.

YOU'LL NEED:
Popsicle sticks, tongue depressors, straws, or twist ties
Screws, nuts, and bolts
Modeling dough or clay
   (see recipe on previous page)

＊ Have your child create a sculpture using the raw materials you've found around the house.

＊ If you plan to hang the sculpture on the wall, put a paper clip on the back in the soft clay before it dries.

YOUR CHILD IS WORKING ON:
Creativity
Resourcefulness
Dexterity

Yarn Pictures

It's like sewing a colorful design!

YOU'LL NEED:
Cardboard or Styrofoam tray
Yarn
Tape
Sharp pencil or paper punch

* Before you and your child begin, wrap the ends of the yarn with tape to make a hard tip that will thread easily.

* Using a paper punch or sharp pencil, make holes in the Styrofoam tray or cardboard.

* Show your child how to thread the yarn through the holes to make designs. He or she may want to use several colors of yarn.

* Encourage your child to try different ways of overlapping the yarn. Threading through the holes may be challenging at first, but you can reassure your child that learning to do careful work with your fingers takes time and practice. This might be an activity that your child does again on other days to see how much easier it becomes with practice.

* Some children might enjoy just drawing dots on paper and joining them in a creative way with a pencil, pen, or marker.

YOUR CHILD IS WORKING ON:
Creativity
Dexterity
Coordination
Persistence

This activity will give your child a creative way to practice the carefully-controlled finger movements that are needed for writing.

Flip-Flap-Fun

Surprises, like the ones under the flaps, can be fun for children when they are in charge of them.

YOU'LL NEED:
Two pieces of construction paper
Blunt-nosed scissors
Tape
Crayons or markers

✳ Give your child one sheet of paper and ask him or her to make a number of squares or rectangles. These boxes will become the "windows" for the other piece of paper.

✳ Using scissors, cut around three sides of each square and have your child help you fold the paper back. The folds can open like windows (vertically) or they can open like doors (horizontally).

✳ Help your child place the other piece of paper under the cut-out paper, connecting the two pieces with a piece of tape at the top for now.

✳ Have your child draw or paste a picture on the bottom sheet under each window.

✳ Tape the papers together on the remaining sides.

✳ Now your child can play "peek-a-boo" with the windows. Your child could also play a "concentration" game in which he or she tries to remember which picture is under which window.

YOUR CHILD IS WORKING ON:
Creativity
Dexterity
Memory

Musical Rhythms

Watch your child capture the rhythm of the music.

YOU'LL NEED:
Rhythmic music on the radio or CD
Paper
Crayons or markers
Play clay (optional)

✳ To help your child focus on the musical beat, start by moving or clapping to the rhythm of the music.

✳ Using the rhythmic beat of the music, have your child move the crayons or markers on paper. Your child might want to make swirls, long or short strokes, or dots according to the rhythm. Lots of interesting designs can emerge when creativity is sparked by the musical beat.

✳ Have your child make another picture to music with a different beat. See how different the design is when the music has changed.

✳ As a variation, your child can use the musical rhythm for play clay fun—tapping on the play clay with fingers, making ridges or other marks on it, or pounding on it.

YOUR CHILD IS WORKING ON:
Creativity
Listening skills

> **This is a different kind of creating because it's inspired by musical rhythms. Instead of focusing on the product, the focus is on the process.**

Make Your Own Fruit Sundae

This sundae isn't made from ice cream; it's made from fruit. Offer a sundae glass or a mug, and let your child make his or her own creation.

YOU'LL NEED:

Sundae glass or mug

Apples, grapes, bananas, oranges, etc.,
    cut in chunks and separated in bowls

Sprinkles

Granola, nuts, cereal, maraschino cherries, etc.,
    for garnish (optional)

Whipped topping or yogurt

✻ Give your child a sundae glass or mug.

✻ Have your child make a sundae creation of his or her own, using the fruit, sprinkles, granola, nuts, maraschino cherries, or any other ingredients you may want to provide.

✻ Top it off with some whipped topping or yogurt, and *Voila!* A healthy treat.

YOUR CHILD IS WORKING ON:

Creativity

Making healthy food choices

Appreciating individual differences

Creative Collages

Colorful tissue paper can be an especially inviting material for creative play.

YOU'LL NEED:

Tissue paper in several colors
Tray or shoe box
Cotton swabs or small brushes
Liquid starch or diluted glue
Plain paper for the background

* Have your child tear the tissue paper into small bits, using a tray or shoebox to hold all the pieces.

* Using cotton swabs or small brushes, let your child paint the background paper with liquid starch or diluted glue (half glue, half water) and then arrange the tissue paper pieces on the sticky paper to create a design or picture.

* Your child might also want to make a similar collage with scraps of wrapping paper, wallpaper, greeting cards, or bits of magazine pictures or yarn.

YOUR CHILD IS WORKING ON:
Creativity
Dexterity

Paint-a-Cookie

Bring the "artist" into the kitchen for these fun-to-make, fun-to-eat cookies. If you prefer, buy pre-made cookie dough to make the project even easier!

YOU'LL NEED:

1 package of pre-made sugar cookie dough, or one batch of sugar cookie dough from a recipe

4 cups sifted confectioners' sugar

⅓ cup water

Food coloring

Pastry brush

Several small bowls

New clean paint brushes

✳ Bake the cookies and let them cool.

✳ Whisk together confectioners' sugar and ⅓ cup water, adding up to 2 tablespoons more water if necessary to make the icing smooth enough to spread.

✳ Divide remaining icing among the small bowls and tint each one with different food colorings depending on how many icing colors your child wants to use. Thin the icing slightly with more water if necessary.

✳ Your child can paint the cookies, using the pastry brush or paint brushes to decorate the cookies.

✳ Let the cookies dry completely before storing in airtight containers.

YOUR CHILD IS WORKING ON:
Creativity
Following directions
Dexterity

Nature
and Science

Appreciating the world

A mother told me about a walk she had taken with her three year old. "We were just going to the end of the street to the mailbox and back, but it took us a whole morning! Jamilla could have made it an all-day trip! First, she squatted down for a closer look at ants coming out of a crack in the sidewalk. Then she heard some birds above her, so we had to stop while she tried to find where the birds were in the tree. She kicked a stone into a puddle and watched the ripples, and then another stone, and another one! I never knew there was so much to see and do in that one little block between our house and the mailbox!"

Preschoolers are naturally curious creatures. They're engaged in a love affair with the world—as if they've suddenly opened the front door of their home and discovered there's a whole world in front of them. Even the tiniest things become fascinating to them. At this age, they're scientists, observing and experimenting. What a gift it is to us grownups, to see the world through our children's eyes! We might even find that things we took for granted are much more marvelous than we ever thought.

Curiosity and wondering

Children are hungry to know about the world. When we encourage curiosity, we're giving them one of the most important tools they'll need for school, and for life.

After they've mastered language, children often start asking a lot of "why" questions. They are ready to go beyond just naming things to using words to find out more about them. Children recognize that adults seem to know lots of things, so they ask us a lot of questions.

Of course, we don't always have the answers for our children's questions, and sometimes the answers need abstract thinking which is beyond the capacity of preschoolers. I've heard from parents who tell me that at times their children's "why?" questions become exhausting. It's helpful to tell children, "I can't answer that just now.

Let's talk about it later." Or, "I don't know the answer, or how to explain it to you, but that's a really good question." We're still valuing their questions and their appreciation for the world around them.

Attitudes are caught from adults

Just as our children can help to open our eyes to the marvels in the world around us, we can help foster their curiosity and appreciation; like the old Quaker saying: "Attitudes are caught, not taught!" Some of my deep appreciation for nature came from growing up in a small town, where there were many adults around who had a sense of wonder and respect for nature. I'll never forget my walks in the woods with my Grandfather McFeely. Birds, bugs, wildflowers, leaves, streams—they all remind me of the joys of being with him.

Haven't you found that one of the best ways children learn is from the example of the grownups they love? When children see that you wonder about and care for living things, when you marvel at a sunset or the moon on a particular night, that lets them know that you appreciate nature. And it's often quite contagious!

How Do Plants Drink?

Does your child know how plants get food?

YOU'LL NEED:
Celery stalks (including leaves)
Water
Jar or glass
Food coloring
Drinking straws (optional)

✳ Cut off about 1 inch from the bottom of a stalk of celery and show your child the little holes in the stalk. They are like skinny straws, packed closely together. Explain that the celery plant draws water up through the holes, the way we drink from a straw.

✳ Put some food coloring in a jar of water, and then put the celery stalk in the jar of colored water. After a few hours, the top leaves will begin to turn the same color as the water. Cut one of the celery stalks in half, and your child may be able to see the colored water in the veins.

✳ Now that your child has seen "celery straws" at work, you may want to put out drinking straws for water or juice at the next meal.

YOUR CHILD IS WORKING ON:
Awareness of science (learning how a plant takes in water)
Observation skills
Curiosity

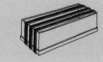

Leaf Rubbings

Here's an activity that gives your child a different way to look at leaves.

YOU'LL NEED:
Several leaves from different trees or plants
Lightweight paper
Crayons

✳ Put a leaf under a piece of paper and show your child how to rub across it with the side of a crayon. Hold the leaf and paper still while rubbing the crayon across the paper. See how the outline appears, as if by magic. Rub some more, and you'll see the veins of the leaf.

✳ Try this rubbing technique with several different kinds of leaves. Ask your child to look closely at what is different about each of the leaf rubbings. Do some have jagged edges? Smooth edges? Do they have a stem going up the center? Do they have veins? What is similar about all the leaves?

✳ This activity can be a matching game, too. Can your child match the leaves with the rubbings?

YOUR CHILD IS WORKING ON:
Observation skills
Recognizing likeness and difference
Appreciating nature

As you help your child see similarities *and* differences in the leaves, you can also talk about how people are alike and different. Appreciating people is part of appreciating the world.

Homemade Toothpaste

Invite your child to play "scientist" and mix chemicals to make toothpaste.

YOU'LL NEED:
4 teaspoons baking soda
1 teaspoon salt
1 teaspoon flavoring (vanilla, almond, or peppermint extract)
Toothbrush
Air-tight container

✳ Mix the ingredients together to make homemade toothpaste.

✳ Dentists generally recommend that children brush their teeth for a minute or two. You might want to think of a familiar song to hum that takes that long, then sing it as your child brushes his or her teeth.

✳ Be sure to cover the container with a tight-fitting lid after each use.

YOUR CHILD IS WORKING ON:
Awareness of science
Dental health
Responsibility
Curiosity

This activity can give you an opportunity to talk with your child about what we do to care for our teeth, like:
• brushing in the morning and before bedtime
• brushing after meals (when we can)
• flossing to get out bits of food and to keep our gums healthy
• brushing or rinsing after eating sweet and sticky foods
You might find that your child pays more attention to dental care and brushing because you've worked together to make your own toothpaste.

Pumpkin Seeds

Children love to know about "hidden treasures" that are inside of things. Open a pumpkin and what do you find inside? Seeds that can turn into tasty toasted treats!

YOU'LL NEED:
Ripe pumpkin
Sharp knife
Large spoon
Paper towels
Vegetable oil
Cookie sheet
Oven
Salt (optional)

✳ Cut open the pumpkin and scoop out the seeds.

✳ Wash the seeds under running water, then spread them on paper towels to dry.

✳ Shake salt on the seeds, if you wish.

✳ Spray or spread oil on the cookie sheet. Then scatter the seeds on the cookie sheet.

✳ Bake in a 250°F oven for at least an hour for the seeds to dry out completely. Shake the seeds a few times. If you want, you can turn up the heat to brown the seeds for a few minutes, but be careful because they burn easily.

✳ Remove the seeds from the cookie sheet. Store in an airtight container so the seeds stay crisp.

YOUR CHILD IS WORKING ON:
Awareness of science (learning about seeds)
Curiosity
Following directions
Patience

Tele-Cups

Sounds can travel along a tight string. As the string vibrates, an earpiece on the other end will pick up the sound and make it louder, kind of like a telephone. Of course, the most important parts of a telephone call are the people who are talking!

YOU'LL NEED:

2 Styrofoam or paper cups, or containers from frozen juice or yogurt
Sharp pencil or nail
3' to 6' of string

✳ Poke a hole in the bottom of the cups with pencil or nail.

✳ Help your child thread the string through the holes. Knot the string inside the cups.

✳ Because the vibration of the string is what makes the phones work, make sure that the string is as tight as possible.

✳ Your child may want to experiment with Styrofoam *and* paper cups to see which one lets the sound travel better.

YOUR CHILD IS WORKING ON:

Awareness of science (learning about vibration)
Cooperation
Creativity

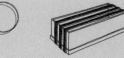

Shoebox Guitar

Show your child how to turn science into music.

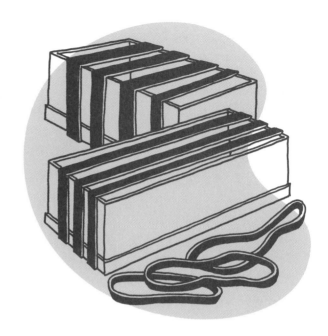

YOU'LL NEED:
Shoebox (without the lid)
3 or 4 rubber bands of different sizes

✶ Help your child stretch the rubber bands across the width of the shoebox, and then show your child how to pluck or strum the rubber bands. The different sizes of rubber bands should make different sounds. You might even want to create an entire string section of a pretend orchestra using different sized boxes and rubber bands.

✶ You may want to add a cardboard tube to one end of the box to make it look like a guitar.

YOUR CHILD IS WORKING ON:
Creativity
Awareness of science (learning about
   vibration)
Listening skills
Recognizing likeness and difference

> It's more than music you'll be making: you'll be encouraging an appreciation of sounds and science, helping your child develop listening skills, and most important of all, sharing some time together.

Let's Take a Walk

Children can find all kinds of treasures everywhere.

YOU'LL NEED:
A place to walk (sidewalk, yard, or trail)
Small bag or box (optional)
Magnifying glass (optional)

✳ Plan a walk with your child. You may not get very far, or move very quickly, but your child can have a chance to look for things like:

> Leaves, flowers, or plants
> Tiny bugs or stones
> Squirrels, dogs, or cats

✳ If your child likes to collect things, bring along a small bag to gather things that you find along the way. When you're back home, those things might become part of a collage or a mobile. Leaves can be used in rubbings. Stones can be painted and used as paperweights. Your child might want to keep the collection in a "treasure box" like a shoe box.

✳ Children who are interested in trees might enjoy a "tree walk." Help your child get to know the trees on your walk. Look carefully at their shapes and sizes. Touch the bark. Look at the shapes of different leaves.

✳ If your child is an explorer, take along a magnifying glass for close examinations.

YOUR CHILD IS WORKING ON:
Appreciating nature
Observation skills
Curiosity

When adults go for a walk, we're usually on our way somewhere, and we walk at a steady pace. When children go for a walk, they stop and look at things around them. In fact, for them, looking is far more important than walking.

A Windowsill Garden

Most plants grow very slowly, and children don't have the patience to wait for a plant to grow. Here are some plants that grow rather quickly, so your child can see changes in a few days or a week.

YOU'LL NEED:

3 or 4 dried beans
Paper towels
Glass jar with lid
Water

✳ Soak the dried beans overnight in some water. This will make the beans grow faster.

✳ Line a jar with damp paper towels.

✳ Place 3 or 4 dried beans between the towels and the jar so you can see them through the sides of the glass.

✳ Keep the paper towels damp by adding a little bit of water to the bottom of the jar each day, as needed.

✳ Check the seeds from time to time for signs of growth.

✳ Within a week, the beans should sprout and start to grow. Eventually, leaves will begin to grow on the stem. Your child could make a chart to graph the height of the stem.

✳ If it's spring or summer, your child could plant the sprouts outdoors when the plants are about 2 inches tall. Your child can watch for changes that take place outdoors—more leaves, blossoms, and tiny beans. If the beans grow large enough, your child can open one and look at the new bean seeds inside.

YOUR CHILD IS WORKING ON:

Awareness of science (learning about growing)
Appreciating nature
Curiosity
Patience

Shiny Pennies

Watch a dirty penny turn into a shiny one.

YOU'LL NEED:
Several dull and dirty pennies
¼ cup white vinegar
1 teaspoon salt
Clear, shallow bowl (not metal)
Paper towels
Nickel

✳ Put the salt and vinegar in the bowl. Stir until the salt dissolves.

✳ Put the pennies in the liquid and watch them go from dirty to clean.

✳ Rinse the pennies well under running water. Set them on the paper towel to dry.

✳ Have your child then try this experiment with a nickel. You'll find that the nickel won't react in the same way as the penny because it lacks copper, the element that causes this chemical reaction to take place.

YOUR CHILD IS WORKING ON:
Awareness of science (chemical reactions)
Curiosity

When we help children understand that the cause-and-effect relationships of science are predictable, they feel more secure and appreciate that the wonders of the world aren't just magic. One reason this experiment is great for young children is that there's a fairly simple explanation for why the copper gets shiny. Over time, the copper in a penny mixes with oxygen in the air and makes the copper dull in color. In the acidic vinegar solution, the copper separates from the oxygen, restoring its shine.

Me and My Shadow

Take advantage of a sunny day and go out searching for shadows.

✻ Go outside into the sunshine with your child. Ask your child to look for his or her shadow. What happens when your child moves? Can your child make the shadow dance?

✻ Look for shadows of different objects—cars, telephone poles, street signs, trees.

✻ You might want to share the classic poem, "My Shadow" by Robert Lewis Stevenson. Here's the first verse:

> I have a little shadow who goes in
>   and out with me
> And what can be the use of him is
>   more than I can see
> He is very, very like me from my
>   heels up to my head
> And I see him jump before me when
>   I jump into my bed.

✻ If you can, go outdoors again later on and see what your child's shadow looks like at a different time of the day. Where is the shadow? What does it look like?

YOUR CHILD IS WORKING ON:
Curiosity
Observation skills
Awareness of science (learning about the effect of sun light)
Literacy

Index by Name of Activity

T

W

Y

Index by Type of Activity

This index is helpful for when you want to focus on a specific area of your child's development, or for when you're looking for an activity to fill a certain need. Here, the activities are listed by developmental benefits and by descriptive categories. For instance, if you are looking for something to do outside, you can look under "outside play;" if you are looking for an activity to encourage your child to read, check "literacy" for some suggestions.

A

E

F

M

N

Things to Save

Babyfood jars

Bottle caps

Boxes (cereal, pudding, cracker, etc.)

Calendars

Cardboard

Cardboard tubes (paper towel, toilet paper)

Catalogs

Cotton

Detergent bottles

Egg cartons

Empty spools of thread

Fabric scraps

Grocery bags

Jar lids

Magazines

Margarine containers

Newspaper

Paper bags

Paper clips

Popsicle sticks

Socks

Sponges

String

Styrofoam or cardboard meat and
    vegetable trays

Styrofoam packing material

Tin, plastic, and cardboard containers of
    all shapes

Used wrapping paper

Wood scraps

Yarn

Yogurt containers

About the Author

Fred McFeely Rogers is best-known as "Mister Rogers," creator and host, composer and puppeteer for the longest running program on PBS, *Mister Rogers' Neighborhood.*

His journey to the "Neighborhood" began in 1950, during his senior year at Rollins College, when he became intrigued by the potential of children's television. After graduating from Rollins, he headed to NBC as an assistant producer for *The Kate Smith Hour* and *The Voice of Firestone.* In 1952, he married Joanne Byrd, a pianist and fellow Rollins graduate.

Returning to his hometown area of western Pennsylvania in 1953, he helped found Pittsburgh's public television station, WQED, and co-produced the hour-long live daily children's program *The Children's Corner* for which he also worked behind-the-scenes as puppeteer and musician. It was on *The Children's Corner* that several regulars of today's *Mister Rogers' Neighborhood* made their first appearances— among them, Daniel Striped Tiger, King Friday XIII, X the Owl, and Lady Elaine Fairchilde.

To broaden his background for children's television, Fred Rogers studied at the University of Pittsburgh's Graduate School of Child Development. He also completed a Bachelor of Divinity degree at the Pittsburgh Theological Seminary and was ordained as a Presbyterian minister in 1963 with a unique charge of serving children and families through the media.

Mister Rogers' Neighborhood made its national debut on public television in 1968. Since then, this pre-eminent series has been recognized internationally as a unique and pioneering effort to communicate with young children about things that matter in childhood. *TV Guide* says " . . . *Mister Rogers' Neighborhood* makes us, young and old alike, feel safe, cared for, and valued. . . . wherever Mister Rogers is, so is sanctuary." Fred Rogers has been the recipient of virtually every major award in television and education, and has received honorary degrees from more than 38 colleges and universities.

Fred Rogers is the Chairman of the Board of Family Communications, Inc., the nonprofit company that he formed in 1971 to produce *Mister Rogers' Neighborhood.* The company has since diversified into non-broadcast materials that reflect the same philosophy and purpose: to encourage the healthy emotional growth of children and their families.

Play is the expression of our creativity, and creativity, I believe, is at the very root of our ability to learn, to cope, and to become whatever we may be.

—Fred Rogers